D0297248

A BROTHER'S
JOURNEY

A BROTHER'S JOURNEY

Surviving a Childhood of Abuse

Richard B. Pelzer

timewarner
books

A *Time Warner* Book

First published in the United States of America by Warner Books in 2005
First published in Great Britain by Time Warner Books in 2005
Reprinted 2005 (twice)

A CIP catalogue record for this book is available from the British Library.

ISBN 0 316 72732 6

Printed and bound in Great Britain by Clays Ltd, St Ives plc

Time Warner Books
An imprint of
Time Warner Book Group UK
Brettenham House
Lancaster Place
London WC2E 7EN

www.twbg.co.uk

This work is dedicated to all of us who have been through an experience such as this. We are not survivors nor are we victims. We are the ones that were given a chance to experience life as few people ever will. We are tempered and made stronger in our foundations through the fire we once knew. The embers that often bring back the memories and tears will always burn. They are a reminder of where we once were. As responsible and productive adults, we now have the opportunity to share, understand, and even heal. We must always remember and admit that this happens to children we know and children we don't. This happens every day and often in our own neighborhoods. This work is dedicated to all those that step up and make our homes the loving safe haven they should be. I admire and I am inspired by your dedication.

ACKNOWLEDGMENTS

I would like to thank my wife, Joanne; my agent Jim Schiavone, Ed.D.; my editor John Aherne; Mr. and Mrs. Digby Diehl; Angie Wilks-Grace of America ISP; Mr. and Mrs. Dave Pelzer; the staff at D'Esprite; John and Darlene Nichols; Lori Lutz; Judy Hansen; and Paula Boggs.

CONTENTS

INTRODUCTION

I tried to hide the secrets of my past from my wife for as long as I could. I revealed my fears and tears only to the pages in my personal journal. I just couldn't bring myself to tell my own wife, face-to-face, about my past and who I was back then. I tried to hide any scars and personal habits that would give away the secrets I lived with.

Early in our marriage, however, I experienced both embarrassment and shame that I thought I would never get over. My wife found what I had tried so desperately to hide.

I was resting in the front room when it happened. Rest is different for me than for other people. Often in our early marriage, whenever I was tired or overly burdened with some concern on my mind, I would rest with a blanket wrapped around my head. The purpose of the blanket was to cover my face and hide the secret from anyone who looked at me.

Some twenty-three years earlier I had perfected the ability to sleep with my eyes open and be aware of any movement within my line of vision. It was an alarm system I used when I "slept." Often as a child, I was able to bring myself back into consciousness if I saw Mom cross my line of vision as she walked into my room at night. It was a safety mechanism.

For so long I answered my wife's repeated questions as best I could without giving away the truth. I lied and said that it was insecurity and I would eventually grow out of it.

In one day that all changed. I was caught and couldn't lie my way out of it any longer. I was resting without my blanket around my head.

I saw her as she walked into the front room. I saw her as she approached me resting and looked at me. I was aware that she was there, but I failed to bring myself back into consciousness fast enough when she looked at me. She looked into my eyes as if I was wide awake. I lay there motionless, in between asleep and waking. Somewhere in the middle is where I find my rest.

Her reaction was what I had always feared. She assumed I was dead.

Within a moment I was awake and responding to her reaction. I immediately sat up and looked at her. I was at a loss for words and said nothing at first.

It's difficult to find the words to explain what I felt at that moment. I was ashamed. I was stuttering some meaningless statement when I realized that it was futile. She had seen my eyes as I slept, and nothing I could say would ever change the image now burned in her memory. We both simply waited for the other to respond. The silence only added to the tension and confusion.

All I wanted was to comfort my wife. All I wanted was the chance to try to explain.

After a few moments I answered as many questions as I could. I knew that she wouldn't understand without knowing far more about my background than I had ever told her. Now I had the chance to pay my penance and repair the damage my silence had caused. She reacted with compassion and understanding. On the surface I was relieved to share something so personal with the one I loved. Inside I was confused and felt the same emotion I hid as a child—shame. For a moment I was that little boy again, that little boy who had been horribly abused. I became that child who found comfort in silence and warmth in solitude. As I sat with my wife and we talked, I began to realize that she held a deeper love for me than I knew possible. At that moment she was, and to this day remains, my other half.

I had always found my journal to be a relief for me. I wrote in it for years. I realized that my past needed to be kept silent. No one could know who I was back then.

My journal allowed me to expel the emotions and hurt on pages that remained silent. No one would ever read them and experience the emotions I hid from the world. Taking pen to paper was a safe way for me to begin the healing process.

As I reviewed particular times in my life, though, I found that there was a message in the feelings of a once timid and shy little boy who grew to be the person I am today.

Nine years after we were married, my wife and I decided to publish these memoirs in the hope that its experiences and lessons will help readers understand. There are lessons in life that we all have to experience for ourselves. There are other lessons that we can learn from others, lessons that spare us the pain and cost of experience. The lessons I learned and my experiences in this book are very private, and yet I hope they have the power to open hearts and help heal wounds for others.

I realized the value in these memoirs as my wife sat beside me and we worked through the tears and the fear that surfaced as I went deeper and deeper into the place that once held these secrets.

At times I was unable to read a paragraph or even a sentence I had written without breaking into tears. She had known of only a few of the experiences I'd had and the way they affected me. Before writing this book I kept those emotions hidden. Now I don't have to hide them anymore. I can allow them their place in my heart. I found that the more I was able to share, the more my wife and I were able to work together to make this a better book, with a stronger purpose.

When this project was finished, I finally realized the impact child abuse has and the lifelong effect on its victims.

Child abuse affects far more than the victim. It affects generations.

Each of us who has suffered child abuse deals with it differently. I'm fortunate to have a wonderful wife and her powerful love. She may not know all the little things she does to help me, but as I grow and feel better about myself, I'm able to share more and more. It's as if we fall in love over and over again. She is my rock and my comforting pillow at the same time.

My life has changed for the better now that I'm able to live with the truth. I'm able to control my feelings, and I know where they belong in my heart. Before this book, I was only able to prevent them from surfacing. Now I find that I don't have to control that anymore; I can live with them in harmony with my daily life. I understand that these feelings and thoughts are part of who I am.

Sharing this story has been therapeutic for me and has brought me closer to my wife and family. The experiences in this book have touched many lives. It will affect my children when they read about my childhood and understand the drastic difference between the way they were raised and the way I was. It will affect my children's teachers, and their friends and families once the whole story is finally known.

Child abuse affects all of us. Victims are people we work with, live next to, are friends with, and perhaps even live with. They are people who carry the memories of abuse like a stone around their neck.

There are millions of kids in the United States who carry this burden in their hearts and feel that they can't share it with anyone. Even the littlest among us may find it necessary to bury something so painful and so heartbreaking. They bury it deep, where no one can find it. As time goes on, the place where we buried those emotions fills, threatening an eruption.

True peace of mind and heart is something that is earned—something that is worked on and then achieved. It doesn't happen overnight, and it requires the support of those around us who love and want to understand. May all my readers find the true peace of mind and heart that I have found in telling my story.

1

THAT WAS THEN . . .

Daly City, California, 1970

In the beginning, life was fun, life was exciting, and life was good. As a five-year-old, I was tender in age and yet I was cruel and mean. I was happy to watch my brother as he was beaten or forced to perform some disgusting punishment. It was exciting to watch. It is horrifying to remember.

I WANTED TO BELIEVE that we were a middle-class family in a middle-class San Francisco Bay Area suburb. The house was modest, as were all the houses on Crestline Avenue. There were four or five different styles of houses on the street. Each one was painted differently, and yet there was a pattern on the street that reminds me of the famous pastel houses of San Francisco's Rainbow Row. Our house was bright pink. The outside trim was pink; even the concrete steps were pink. Next door had a slightly different layout and was painted in two tones of brown. As you walked down the street, the colors of the houses would eventually repeat themselves to form a pattern. Every family on the street had pride in their yards and their houses.

There were two dozen kids on the street, and most of them were within a few years of me in age. The boys all had bicycles and who knows what the girls had. Who cared? They were girls. They didn't play football, basketball, or dodgeball; they were just girls. The boys would often ride bikes around the street in packs. Mostly to show off the new seats or handlebars they just got.

I recall particular early memories about Mom but very few about Dad. He just was seldom there. He was almost invisible. I remember Dad occasionally being in the house, but always in the background. I don't know if he had already moved out or if he was just never there anymore. It's almost as if he was a tenant, not participating in the lives of his kids. I'm not sure if it was always that way. Perhaps before I came along things were different. Maybe Dad and Mom were happy then. Maybe they were a real family then. I don't know. I don't have many other memories about my father. I simply didn't know him.

Mom made a show of nurturing "tradition" and "family." She worked very hard at making elaborate dinners and setting the table with Hawaiian tablecloths or Chinese dishes, stemware, and tableware, depending on what she created for dinner. I used to love sitting at the table with my own Chinese teapot and decorative dishes that only I used. Each of us had a set, and each one was a different pattern and color from the rest. Those table settings always made each of us feel special. From Hawaiian to Chinese to German themes and cuisine,

Mom made dinner a special event. The table was usually set better than in most restaurants in San Francisco. Candles, linen napkins, and silver always made the dining table sparkle.

One of my best memories was constantly fighting with my younger brother, Keith, over a certain table setting. Whenever dinner was just plain baked ham, sweet potatoes, bread, corn, and applesauce, the table was set with the everyday dishes. There was one particular plate that had a chip out of the flower pattern and one fork that had a line near the top of the handle, as if something had melted a mark across the handle. Over the years Keith and I would fight over who would set the table. The rivalry over whose seat was set with the broken plate and fork was never-ending. Always in fun, but completely serious, we would swap knives and plates ten times behind each other's backs—even after the table was set. We mocked each other in defeat as dinner eventually started. The victor (whichever one of us ended up with the "broken fork" or "broken plate") shamelessly repeated:

"I got the broken fork. I got the broken fork."

Drive-in movies were always special events. One of the first movies I recall seeing was Disney's *Bambi* at the drive-in, and I was happy with the togetherness we shared as brothers. But camping was even more fun. We camped as a family— Mom, Ross, Scott, Keith, and me. Dad never camped with us, and I recall David on a camping trip only once. Nonetheless, their absence didn't change the fact that "the family" was camping. The five of us were "the family."

Mom had a habit of spontaneously announcing that we were going. Within two hours of the announcement, Mom and the boys had the car loaded and were off to one of the local campgrounds. Ross, Scott, Keith, and I would be sitting in the car waiting for Mom in high anticipation. It was always fun to be spontaneous; so many of my camping memories are vibrant and so real that they seem as if they occurred only yesterday. But sometimes, when I think back to those times, I can't recall the color of our sleeping bags or the color of the tent.

Some weekends, Mom would take us on day trips to the beach. The drive to Thornton Beach on the Pacific Ocean was short; it was only about twenty minutes from our house. The anticipation was too much for any five-year-old, and was overwhelming for me at that age. The beach was one of the few places we went as a family in public and were allowed to exercise the normal relationships shared among most brothers. Tossing a football from brother to brother was always part of the beach experience for us, and deliberately skipping one brother's turn just to start a fight was inevitable. Ross was about eleven, Scott was about eight, and Keith was a newborn.

When I think back to when all of us were living together, it is not clear if there were five boys or four. It was normal for Ross, Scott, and myself to be involved in some sport or game or brotherly challenge. David was rarely there. He was never allowed to play or speak to us. He was expected to be silent and only watch as the other boys played and shared with one another. Sometimes I remember David being there, and other times I don't. So many times he was left behind in the house, just not part of our daily lives. He was part of the background—something that you know is there but isn't important.

It has been difficult for me to force myself to remember David because I have buried those memories for so many years. As an adult, I am shocked to remember what was being done in that house. I am deeply ashamed of my own childhood participation in the horrific events. From my earliest memories, unspeakable acts of violence were happening in our family that I couldn't understand at the time. As a child, I didn't know that these acts never should have happened or been allowed to happen. The violence was a part of daily life before I can even remember.

The harsh truth is, my childhood was a lie. Beneath the surface our family was anything but normal. There were horrible secrets in the backs of each of our minds. We all knew what they were and yet never talked about them. We were afraid to.

2

GOOD BOY

Children can be very cruel to each other in an ignorant and often uncivilized manner. But when an adult—a parent—encourages, nurtures, and even rewards such behavior, the cruelty becomes perverted. Mom demanded that all "her boys" had to treat their brother David as something less than human. In her own twisted formulation, she singled me out to be her particular informer, her co-conspirator, against him. At thirty years' distance from my cruelty, I still cringe with shame at my participation in his pain and degradation. I was five years old and I was trying to survive within a crazy scheme of rules enforced by my mother. Despite my adult disgust for my own childhood acts, I have tried to tell the truth about what happened in that house as honestly as I can remember. The strongest thought I recall when I reflect back on my childhood was simply Eat or be eaten.

I DON'T KNOW WHY Mom and Dad were married. The few times I asked about Dad, she never said anything about him. She just refused to talk about him. Mom had made him mysterious to me.

At first, I think they were happy together. I used to look at Mom's wedding picture, and I remember looking at her like she was the most beautiful girl I had ever seen. She was like a star from the really old movies on TV. She seemed happy to be near such a tall man as Dad. He was well over six feet tall and had dark hair. He was defiantly handsome. The few times I looked through old photo albums, I felt a sense of pride in the photos of Mom and Dad. They had such good-looking friends who were always laughing and enjoying life. Most of the photos showed Dad with a drink or a cigarette in his hand surrounded by friends and family. Mom would often have a drink in her hand and cigarette in her mouth and was also surrounded by friends. I didn't know any of the names or the faces but I felt as though I should. Uncle This and Uncle That is all I was told. None of them was an uncle by blood, just by friendship, and none of them ever came by the house after the kids came along.

Mom grew up in Salt Lake City and was very much a so-cialite. She would tell stories of friends and family she re-membered enjoying. Dad was slightly older than Mom and could have had his pick of brides based on the looks and charm that are evident in old photos. I have no idea where he grew up or what kind of family he came from. I have no idea if he had brothers or sisters, or if his parents are still alive. I have no idea where he was born. He was a stranger to me. That's just what Mom wanted. She wanted me and the other boys to be dependent on her. That way she was in complete control.

I recall a few relatives saying that "Steve could have had his pick of them and that Cathy wouldn't settle for anyone else."

"All she wanted was Steve."

"They're perfect for each other."

Mom often went by the name Cathy. She told me once that it was a nickname her friends had stuck her with years before. Her given name, Roerva, was derived from the first few letters of her family members' names: Ruth, Ott, and Ervan.

Dad was just Steve—strong in his stance and larger than life in the old photos, Dad was, well, Dad. In many ways I thought of the two them as being "cool"—in the photos, anyway. They looked like they had it all together and were the perfect couple.

By the time I came along, some six years after the first boy, the excitement of having children must have worn off. Four boys in a row must have made Dad proud, but I think it made Mom tired.

Sure enough, another brother was soon added to the litter. In many ways I think having kids sort of interrupted Mom's lifestyle. Once the parties became late nights with toddlers and homework, the luster of having kids was tarnished with the memories of more exciting times.

Somewhere in the middle of this family, something was different. Something was, well, wrong. Around the age of five, I understood that there was a difference between *the boys* and *the boy.* Between Ross and Scott there was another boy, a child I knew by many names:

"Him."

"The Boy."

"IT."

"David."

I was taught to hate him as early as I can remember. He was supposed to be a horrible child, an embarrassment to the family, deserving of every form of abuse he received. Mom called him:

"The freak."

"A miserable excuse for a human being."

"The thing that's lucky to be alive."

He was like some animal you see on scary late-night television shows that's kept under the steps, and yet the rest of the family seems normal.

He was a fearful boy. He was dreadfully skinny, wore pitiful rags, and smelled horrible, since he wasn't allowed to bathe. He had a habit of staring at you with eyes that looked past you as if there was no life left in them. And that's what frightened me the most about him, those eyes—those incredibly empty eyes.

He lived in the basement and wasn't allowed to speak. He was rarely permitted to wash, and was fed only leftovers a few times a week. He had many chores to do around the house, which he had to complete quietly and within the time limits set by Mom in order to avoid the consequences of her rage.

Occasionally he was allowed enough time to complete his chores and was rewarded with food, scraps mostly, but food nonetheless. During the time that he lived with us I was young and never thought too much about why he was treated that way. Things were just the way they were and there was no sense trying to understand them. Mom had told us often that he was a terrible boy and that he was a shame to our family. She told us that he constantly committed all sorts of unpardonable crimes, and that he had to pay for them. I don't think I ever actually believed that. I couldn't imagine when he would have time to commit those crimes.

Up to this point Mom kept the focus of her severe abuse on David, but occasionally she was abusive to the other boys as well. Never anything like what David went through. I was too young to know the difference between abuse and punishment. Yet I knew that what David went through was different from what I saw the rest of us go through. Different from anything I had ever experienced up to that point. As long as David was still around, I felt almost safe, knowing that Mom would much rather beat him senseless or abuse David than me.

Living in such a house, each of us understood that there was a need to watch out for each other, and yet it was almost every man, or boy, for himself. I knew what was happening to my brother David. I saw the way Mom punished him for the simplest mistake. She was capable of abusing her children in ways that most people couldn't even dream of. As brothers we were afraid of her. I was terrified of her. All we had as kids was each other. We had to stick together.

We were like a wolf pack. Even though we stuck together, we were able to turn on one another without hesitation or remorse. It was almost as if we had to make sure that, individually, we stayed out of the way and were invisible at times. The alternative to being invisible was to watch and often participate in the destruction of one of the pack, at least when we were in the house and Mom was near. When one of us was mad at another brother all we had to do was tattle; whether the story was true or false didn't matter. It wasn't much different from any other sibling relationship. Tattling and making up stories about what a brother did to get you in trouble goes on in any normal family. What was so abnormal was the way Mom reacted. Getting repeatedly slapped and kicked for calling my older brother a "retard" was not only normal for me, it was expected. I knew what Mom would do to me the second I called him that.

At the time, I didn't really think I was being abused. When I compared what my brother went through to what I went through, I was actually lucky—up until the state took him away.

Outside the house we took on the role of brothers and stuck together in secrecy. Ross would always watch out for me and carefully ensure that I was safe and secure. Ross and I had an unspoken agreement: We would never turn on one another. Scott and I had no such understanding. We were intentionally destructive toward one another. Any chance I had I would call him a "retard" just to get him back for whatever it was he'd said or done to me.

As far as IT was concerned, he was free game. He was available to be blamed, punished, or even devoured, much the way wolves would do.

We all were superior to IT, and I used that to my advantage. It was almost as if IT was a dog that I was allowed to kick at will. He was an animal that I could abuse. I could force him to feel the same lowliness that I was more than used to. It was addictive.

My place, however, was dubious and fragile. In reality, I lived with the constant fear of sliding into the place that he, being IT, occupied. In order to stay where I was, I had to keep him down. I had to contract with Mom to be her "Little Nazi," her ally against IT. I was not only allowed but also encouraged to mistreat him. I was often rewarded for ratting him out to Mom. Ross and I had our pact of protection, but IT and I had a different pact, an unspoken pact of betrayal and lies.

Many times I told on him, knowing full well that Mom would mercilessly beat him, or try once again to kill him. Quite often my accusations were lies, or at least exaggerations of minor faults that in no way required the kind of punishment he received. Nor were those accusations in any way justification for her cruelty. But it was the only way of keeping her hostility focused on IT and away from me. He was my safety valve, a survival tool that I used without any thought whenever I felt that I was in danger. As long as I separated him from me, I was safe and I knew it. I was rewarded for providing Mom with another reason to unleash her fury on him. His life was nothing more than pain and shame. We, as brothers, would separate ourselves from him. Yet my life revolved around ensuring that he was the focus of her madness. Looking back, I don't believe that the other boys ever really wanted to blame him or heighten his flaws. None of my other brothers ever showed any need to have this kind of twisted relationship with Mom. None of my brothers ever took advantage of Mom's twisted way of punishing David. I'm not sure why, but I found a comfort in degrading David and making him the focus of Mom's anger. It was the only thing I had to hang on to and I wasn't about to give it up or share it with anyone, at any price. Being able to get IT in more trouble than me was all I had. I remember the times that he suffered because of me, and I was, and am to this day, flooded with guilt and regret.

At first it was just for the sake of keeping him down to protect myself. But as time went on, I grew desperate. I was desperate to once again taste the bitter sweetness of causing him harm. In many ways my anger as a child was satisfied when I watched or listened to his cries of pain as Mom beat him senseless for some lie I told. Often she would beat him for his failure to complete chores to meet "our" expectations. I was part of her and the madness she lived. I, too, lived for it. I recall speaking to IT as if I had her full support in degrading him. I didn't need her permission. I had her confidence. I was on her side and I lived for the chance to get him in trouble.

Whenever Mom was abusing my brother, I was always afraid that she would do the same to one of us—or, more specifically, me. It wasn't as if any of the rest of us was spared from Mom's abuse. I was often slapped around, kicked, abusively spanked for the simplest and most meaningless flaws.

It's hard to understand, but at the time I thought that Mom was "abusive" to David and simply "disciplining" the rest of us. Once David left the house, that abruptly changed.

I remember the day Mom caught me walking up the stairs from the basement long before she had announced that I was permitted to get out of bed. She had very strict rules about that: No one was allowed to get up in the morning without her permission. I must have been five years old at the time.

The night before, Mom had been in a frenzy; she had been drinking and walking the house all night. I had been careful to stay out of her way. I was afraid she would vent her frustrations on me. I had gone to bed in silence after my evening chores, and had lain awake with the covers pulled over my head. I expected her come in my room, and I waited for hours.

She had the habit of walking into my room at night to say good night. I knew that if I did anything wrong—if I was awake when she wanted me to be asleep, if I was asleep when she wanted me to be awake, or if I gave the wrong answer to a certain question—she would explode and hurt me. Being in the mood she was in that night, I was sure there would be trouble.

I froze with fear when I finally heard the door open later that night. I heard the sound of her heavy steps as she approached me where I lay on the upper bunk bed in my room. I was expecting her to pull the covers off my head, bellow something at me, or simply start hitting me, but nothing happened. I waited and waited—everything was perfectly still. I strained for any sign of her presence: her breathing, the creaking of the wooden floor as she sneaked out of my room, anything that could tell me that she was either there or had gone. It was incredibly hot under the blankets and I was desperate to breathe, but I didn't dare move. If she was there, she would hurt me if I moved. So I lay there for hours in silence and the immobility I had perfected. Petrified with fear and the uncertainty of not knowing whether she had left or was just playing another one of her cruel games, I counted the minutes, as many as I could. I wasn't sure what came after thirty and I would start over and over again. Eventually exhaustion overtook me and I fell asleep.

In the morning I woke up soaked in my own sweat and urine. It wasn't the first time. It actually happened to me often and, as usual, I panicked at the thought that she would know that I had once again wet my bed.

I was just too scared of what she might do if she caught me leaving my bedroom and making my way to the bathroom during the night. There simply wasn't enough room in my heart for that kind of courage. I couldn't do it. I was too afraid to walk to the bathroom without her permission.

I slipped quietly out of my bed, removed the sheets, and replaced them with new ones. I headed toward the door carrying the smelly pile of wet linen. I opened the bedroom door slowly, praying that she would still be sleeping. That would allow me time to get down to the basement and leave the sheets in the huge laundry pile. I knew I would have to return later and wash them myself, without her knowing. As I walked carefully down the stairs, inhaling the stench of the sheets, I wondered if I would be allowed to take a shower before school to keep me from smelling like the sheets and becoming, once again, talked about in other children's jokes. It was always the same; I was always cut down and made fun of.

I so desperately wished I could be as cruel to the kids at school as I was to my own brother, IT.

If I was able to lie and force the kids at school to get in trouble, then perhaps I would not get teased or harassed as much. If I could treat the kids at school like I did my brother, then perhaps I could fade away from the spotlight and be ignored, like at home.

Then perhaps they would leave me alone and I could become invisible there, too. At home, Mom always supported my cruelty and harassment of my brother. She helped me become a monster. I was a monster to my brother—IT. No adult at school, or anywhere else, would allow me to be that cruel; no one but Mom. At school, I didn't have the protection of Ross. I was alone and completely vulnerable.

As I walked down the basement stairs I once again was filled with those all-too-familiar feelings of fear and panic. I was familiar with panic and fear. I knew the feeling of being terrified.

The banister was old and wore the dirt of the kids as they held on to it. The steps were covered with black rubber strips for traction yet they were worn beyond being useful. Between the walls and the banister, the few inches of space were always filled with spiderwebs and dust. I was afraid to hang on to it and yet I was afraid not to even more. I knew I had to find the banister with my hands as I carried the pile of urine- and sweat-soaked sheets. I grabbed the banister and felt my hand and arm tremble as I tried to think about something else. I tried to think of neither the spiders nor the webs and walk down one step at a time. I had been awake only a few minutes and I was already sweating. I was sweating fear.

The bottom landing was unstable and I felt as if I would fall through the floor and into some pit that I had yet to discover.

At the bottom of the steps and directly to the left was a small storage area. It was often filled with canned goods and molding potatoes. I recalled the small trapdoor at the far end of this pantry I'd discovered while seeking a new hiding place. I sought safety any chance I had.

The trapdoor opened to a crawl space under the foundation of the house and was only a foot and a half high, just enough for me to hide. The spiders, dirt, and dampness were better than what Mom sometimes had in mind for me.

The basement was a world of its own. Its hard concrete walls were cold and seemed to speak silently of the cruelty and the despair that only they had witnessed. There were mysteries down there, things I hadn't understood as a child. I knew the walls had seen more than I had, and I believed that they contained the fears and emotions that erupted from little boys once they were captured and taken down there. The walls had been absorbing it all for years and years, the true keepers of the secret. The basement was dark and full of boxes of toys that were used during better times. The gray station wagon took up the front half of the basement; the back half was filled with camping gear that knew the same silence that filled that cold and horrific place. All the tents and sleeping bags were covered with cobwebs and home to spiders and insects.

The floor was damp and musty. The smell from our dogs was pungent on the wet cement. I gagged at the odor. There was one light at the bottom of the steps and one other near the car. The back half of the basement was dark and scary. That was where IT lived. I knew that I had to get close to IT to get to the washing machine. Whenever he was in his place in the basement and I had to go down there, I was frightened out of my mind. I didn't know if he would strike out at me from some dark corner of the basement. I was afraid he would try to get me back. I felt alone and powerless in the dark. It was just him and me, and I was now in his world.

IT scared me. I was afraid to look at him. His skeleton-like, bruised body was frightful and his smell was foul, but what scared me more than anything else were those eyes. They had that sheepish yet cunning way of looking at me, like an animal in its hole waiting for some smaller animal to pass its sight. He scared me because I couldn't understand him. And I refused to imagine what it would be like to be him. I just couldn't think about him and how any of us could be him.

He scared me because I knew that I could easily be him. I knew his eyes hid all the fear and all the pain he had endured over the years. I was afraid that if I looked at him and not through him, I would feel some of his pain— or even worse, the pain that I had caused him. I just glanced at him, because as much as he scared me, I also felt sorry for him.

Under the long metal workbench, behind the wood and the tools, I found the sandwich I had hidden there for him the night before. It was only tuna fish and mayonnaise, but it was all I could make for him without being seen by Mom. Sometimes I would secretly hide food, hoping that he would find it. Occasionally I hid the food out of pity. I thought that in some small way it was a way to be forgiven for the times that I deliberately lied about something he'd done. Most of the time, though, I hid food downstairs to be used as a prop when I needed to be her Nazi again. I could count on ratting him out for eating whenever he wasn't allowed to eat.

The sandwich was uneaten and covered with ants. He hadn't seen it. I knew the ants wouldn't have kept him from it. I had seen him eat far worse things before. When he was allowed to, he ate like an animal under the kitchen table next to the dog dish. Sometimes, he ate from the dog dish. The meals we had as a family he spent under the kitchen table while we ate in the dining room. It didn't take long before he taught the dog that he ate first from the bowl on the floor. It was a matter of survival.

I saw him lying there on the green army cot. His eyes stared at me without moving, without thinking or feeling, as if I didn't really exist. Immediately I felt resentment—I was jealous of him. I was jealous because he slept on that army cot, the same one my older brothers used on the few times we went camping. I wasn't allowed to sleep on it. My brothers always had the first choice and now IT had it. It was his bed now.

I envied him and his liberty and thought of him as stupid for not realizing what freedom he had. His world was the basement. He could do whatever he wished there. He could play with the endless objects and toys that were kept there, or he could talk to the cement walls at will without fear of stuttering as I did. He had the "benefit" of silence, though it came from constant fear of being heard by Mom. He had "privileges" such as these that only increased my jealousy further.

I so wished that I could talk to someone, anyone—I found myself resentful of the fact that at least he had the cold concrete walls to talk to.

I quickly dropped the sheets on the laundry pile and was headed back toward the stairs when I glanced at him one more time. The way he looked at me made me angry. All the feelings that Mom had allowed me to discover came to the surface. I was mad, I was really mad.

You're supposed to jump out of bed when one of us is near you! I thought to myself.

It was something that Mom had told me a million times.

He knew that. If I had been Mom, he'd have jumped to his feet and stared at the floor, trembling with fear and respect.

How dare you, I thought.

"Hey, you're supposed to be awake and doing your chores before she gets up. You know that, I'm gonna tell, that'll teach you," I said coldly without even thinking.

The change in him was immediate. There was instant panic in his eyes as he sat up slowly. I could tell that the lesson Mom must have taught him last night was a good one. I basked in the pleasure of seeing him tremble with fear as he attempted to stand up. His body was shaking uncontrollably. I was unsure if it was due to my presence, the threats I had made against him, or his physical condition at the time. It didn't matter. It was all I wanted to see: my shallow superiority over him. I stood there absorbing my fragile glory.

His head hung low and his chin was stuffed into his chest. It was all I needed to see.

I walked up the stairs without looking back at him. A sort of vengeful satisfaction renewed me.

As I went up the stairs toward my room, I relived the recurring nightmare that so often tormented me in my sleep.

In my dream, the stairs would turn into a slide, the banister would disappear, and without anything to hold on to, I would slowly slide toward the monster that waited for me at the bottom of the stairs. As I approached I could hear its laughter, laughter exactly like Mom's. I could feel its claws grabbing my feet and smell its horrible breath. It would seem like hours of struggling and trying to just find enough of a foothold to prevent the inevitable. My dream always ended the same way. I would feel my soul dissolve as I watched the monster's teeth close from inside its mouth and I was swallowed whole.

I couldn't count the times this dream came to me. It was as if I had to learn something from it, but I'd refused to believe what I knew to be its real meaning. I knew exactly what it meant. I just couldn't admit it. I was so involved with my dream that I failed to see her standing at the top of the stairs.

"What the hell are you doing out of bed?" she shouted as she turned on the lights.

Frozen with fear, I stood perfectly still, not knowing what to do.

"Get up here now!" she commanded.

I walked up the stairs with my head hung down. When I reached the top of the steps, she grabbed my chin and forced me to look into her eyes. When she did that, I knew I was in serious trouble.

"I said, what the hell are you doing out of bed?" she repeated.

"IT—he woke me up!" I stuttered.

Only he could arouse that kind of rage in her. Only IT could provoke that kind of fury now in her eyes. Her face reddened with hatred and her eyes became inflamed with determination as she walked past me. She forgot I even existed as she headed down the stairs toward the basement. I stood there filled with horror at what I had just done, cringing as I heard the knocks and the screams coming from the basement. Again I knew that the concrete walls were absorbing the emotions and pain that came from her *private lessons*. The punishment went on and on as if it would never end.

Why do you do that?

These were the confusing thoughts that filled my head. After a moment, I once again realized that I wasn't as superior to IT as I needed to be. I felt ashamed.

Eventually I shrugged it off and tuned out the screams and the images they conjured in my mind. It was a matter of survival. I couldn't allow myself to think too much about it.

I recall one afternoon after school when David was going about his chores. I couldn't pass up the opportunity to try to break him.

I knew that he had arrived home when I heard Mom call him up from the basement and into the kitchen. In order to prove that he hadn't eaten anything during the day she forced him to throw up on the kitchen floor, filter through the mess with his hands, and then clean up after himself. It was disgusting and yet exciting to watch. It was never odd that he was forced to perform such gross acts. He never tried to stand up for himself and none of us, at least not me, ever questioned the way he was treated, at least to Mom's face. It was simply his place and we all accepted it. Many times he was forced to reconsume the mess he had just thrown up. It was awesome to watch. The fear and disgust on his face as he reluctantly forced himself to re-eat what was now thrown up on the floor was addictive. I would watch and wonder if he really was going to do it, although I knew that he would never disobey Mom's commands. It was one of the scariest punishments I ever saw inflicted on him. I was excited to stand there and enjoy the show until I started to think about Mom doing that same thing to me. I had a vague feeling I would eventually take his place someday, and the thought of that took away any of the fun. Now I was scared.

After I watched him clean up his mess, I waited and asked him to follow me to the basement. As usual, he followed quietly, as if he was obeying Mom. The sense of power and the feeling of superiority made the next few moments linger as I basked in pride. Each step I took down the staircase added to the power of being able to command him like some animal Mom was training, and I was testing. By the time I reached the bottom step I was completely filled with a power I can only describe as "raw."

At the bottom of the steps, I lifted my head tall.

"What's that on top of the tools on the floor?" I said.

"I don't know," he replied, ashamed.

He just stood there confused by my question. He knew I was once again about to place him in danger. I looked him over. My eyes traveled up and down his scrawny body. I thought carefully for the next few moments. Making sure not to look into his eyes, I inspected his body and felt shame. Confused, I hesitantly said, "You know that if she finds out that you're eating food you're going to be in trouble?"

His face became frozen as his head sank once again into his chest. It wasn't the first time I had placed him in jeopardy when he was actually completely innocent. His reaction slowly brought me back to the feeling of power over him I was looking for.

"I have to tell, you know. If she finds out I knew and didn't tell she will hurt me," I coldly stuttered at him.

As I looked at him, I recalled the kids at school, and how they mimicked my stuttering and made me feel less than real. And now I was enjoying the same feeling of superiority that I was forced to absorb at school. It was almost a remedy for the day's cruelty.

What I was doing to my brother was exciting, it was powerful, it was necessary for me. Yet it was shameful. I was constantly struggling with the good and the bad feelings that surfaced whenever I was tormenting David. On one hand I was powerful and able to make someone else feel worthless, and on the other hand I felt ashamed and sorry for my actions. It was crazy.

One of Mom's rules that I agreed to follow was to expose any and all of David's flaws. If I didn't, she would get mad and hurt me. The few times I failed to report anything he ever did, I was slapped or spanked for being, as she would say "on his side." I was only six years old. I didn't know what taking sides meant. I didn't know what a twisted web of fear and pain Mom created. She was the master at controlling her children's minds.

The chance to reassure Mom that I was still her faithful informer and report any of David's mistakes was too much to pass up. Even if I had made up the entire event about him eating a sandwich downstairs, I just couldn't pass it by. The comfort I enjoyed was shallow, but all too necessary. It was completely unfair that I felt anything for him or anyone else. I wasn't supposed to feel anything. Not for anyone. Not her, not myself, not the kids at school, anyone. I was supposed to be void of emotion, void of feeling, I was supposed to be her private gestapo and nothing more.

Prior to calling David downstairs with me, I had placed half the sandwich from my lunch box on top of the tools under the workbench. I had taken a bite out of it, as if to show that someone had been eating it. Now I pointed to it, and he slowly lifted his head and realized that once again I had placed him in the way of her wrath.

The sorrow on his face told me I had made him feel just as I wanted him to. The same way I felt at school. I had control over him once again and he knew it. I passed by him, walking toward the steps on my way up to the kitchen to find Mom. He simply stood in the same position; he had to first receive a command to move. As I neared the top of the steps just across from the kitchen, I could see Mom sitting at the table drinking from the gray glass that contained her lifeline— Smirnoff vodka.

Changing the expression on my face from satisfaction to humility, I asked Mom if I could show her something I'd found downstairs. She continued to look at the wall opposite where I was standing, ignoring me. So I laid out my story of deceit, smugly saying, "IT has been eating food! I saw him do it!"

I knew those few words were all I needed to say. Her reaction was as I'd expected. Once she absorbed the meaning of my lie, she finished the glass, slammed it on the tabletop, and then stood up. The look on her face was also what I expected as she walked past me and rubbed my hair, a reward for my evil deeds.

"Good boy, Richard!" she purred.

3

BROTHERS

Some of the most personal things we experience are often shared only between brothers. One brother and I shared a terrible secret that only a few people knew about. I didn't know it at the time, but Mom had carefully created an environment of almost cannibalistic survival. Between my one brother and me, I was the predator and he was the prey.

ONLY A FEW WORDS of betrayal were all I ever needed to keep the "game" going. I knew that if she was happy with my snitching she would not focus on me when she needed to let it all go and release her rage. In some ways it made up for the feeling of worthlessness I was accustomed to at school. This support of my cruelty was the only positive feedback I ever got from Mom, even if it was at my brother's expense. I just couldn't pass up the chance to be thought of in a positive manner. Yet deep down, I knew that it was wrong.

Once she made it to the bottom step, her voice became familiar: evil and cruel.

"I know you're standing there to tell me what Richard found you doing!" she bellowed.

From that point on, I tuned out the rest of what was said and the sounds of slaps echoing up the staircase. Much like a repeat television show, I knew the outcome before the next scene.

There were times when I felt bad about getting him in trouble. This wasn't one of them. I took pleasure and full satisfaction in knowing that I had once again solidified my position with Mom as her Little Nazi.

Another evening, Mom went out with the other kids and left David and me alone in the house. By then I must have been six or seven years old. She often did that. She would take the rest of the kids for an outing and leave me behind. Even when David was still in the house, Mom always made me feel separated from the other kids, by excluding me from a lot of things they did as a family. David was always excluded and Dad was long gone by now.

I walked into her room and found David folding his dirty clothes in piles for the next week. David was seldom allowed anywhere in the house except the basement, under the kitchen table, or in Mom's room. That way, she knew exactly where he was and what he was doing. Folding his clothes was one of his many chores. I decided to have some fun at his expense and to once again show him my place over him. I took the clothes he had just folded and started throwing them around the room.

"I won't take this anymore, Mother!" I screamed, and pretended I was David and was rebelling against her tyranny. In reality, I was rebelling against her, rebelling against him, rebelling against the fear deep inside of becoming him, becoming the replacement.

He got visibly upset, fearing her reaction when she saw the mess in her room. I continued throwing his torn gray briefs all over the room, screaming that I refused to wear them anymore and that there was nothing she could do about it. I was playing out the defiant David that he could never be. All the while he kept pleading with me: "Don't. Please don't!"

I made as much of a mess as I could and was thoroughly enjoying his despair. It made up for the loss of power over him that I had previously felt that morning.

But then I heard his voice become firmer. I suddenly stopped.

"Richard, why are you doing this to me?" he begged.

I looked at him, and his expression wasn't one of anger or fear, just sadness and bewilderment. I looked into those eyes. I was suddenly shaken by an unexpected wave of pity. I felt ashamed.

"I'm sorry," I mumbled.

He looked at me anxiously, trying to figure out whether I was being truthful or just setting him up once again.

"Help me pick up this mess before she gets back?" he asked sincerely.

We folded the clothes together, and for the first time in as long as I could remember, it seemed like we were friends. While we worked I started talking about something. I don't remember what I talked about, probably something entirely irrelevant. But it didn't matter—it was just such a pleasure to be talking to him as a brother for once. There was closeness in those few moments that I could never have dreamed of. Inside I could feel the confusion rise to the surface—the confusion in being a friend to the animal I was sworn to hate.

At some point he interrupted me: "Richard?"

"What?" I asked.

"You haven't stuttered!" he replied.

I looked at him, puzzled.

"No?" I asked. But it was true.

Stuttering had always been a part of my life. It was a curse I had to live with, and I was ashamed of it. Whenever I was in the presence of other people—especially adults—and had to speak, I would get nervous and my words would get tangled in my throat. Now I was happily talking to David as if we were normal kids. At that moment, I felt very grateful to him.

There wasn't a lot of opportunity for gratitude between David and me, and in all honesty I don't think I ever gave him anything to be grateful for. I knew he understood his place in the family and I understood mine. It was shameful and yet acceptable. The memories I have of me being civil to David are few and far between.

Up to this point I knew that Mom would select only David when it came to serious abuse. All the excessive beatings, starvation, and locking him in the bathroom with a pail of cleaning solutions mixed together to create a toxic gas—all those crazy things Mom did to David were specifically done only to him. Somehow I had a feeling that this couldn't go on much longer. I knew that people at school were becoming more and more curious about David. It was just a feeling that I had that he was either going to leave or be taken away. I knew he wasn't going to be around much longer.

Mom never found out about that short but meaningful talk between us, and I keep it in my heart as a cherished memory.

The most vivid memory I have is of the day Mom almost went too far with David. I must have been six or seven years old. As usual, David was eating out of the dog dish under the kitchen table while the rest of the family ate another elaborate meal. If I recall correctly, it was one of the few meals I really hated: prawn shrimp and king crab. I loathed seafood and Mom loved it. I don't think David ever got to even smell any of it.

Lucky him! I thought.

After the meal the rest of the boys went about their business either downstairs or in the front room watching TV. Keith was just a baby, perhaps a year old, and was in his crib in the room he and I shared. The other two boys were quickly out of sight and as usual, Mom was barking out commands to David for cleaning up after her family's dinner. Mom never passed an opportunity to remind David that not only was he *not* part of the family, but he was *not part of anything.*

The three of us were in the kitchen and I struggled to get Mom's attention while she continued to yell commands at him. I felt jealous that David was so much more important to her than I was. I was supposed to be the one she spoke to, not IT.

He was always at the center of her attention. She would stop anything she was doing in order to harass him and yell at him or beat him for whatever reason. It's hard to explain how or why I was jealous of such a thing, but I was starved for attention. I felt so lonely and worthless that I craved any sort of recognition of my existence, even if it was a beating.

She was in one of her moods, and as usual she had been drinking all day. It was now well after six in the evening. My demands for her attention weren't making things any better. She kept screaming at him, telling him to hurry up and work harder. The more I interrupted her, the more worked up she got.

"Work faster! Do you hear me? Work faster! Or I'll kill you!" she screamed.

It wasn't the nasty words or the evil tone of her voice that frightened me, it was the carving knife that she had been holding for a while and kept waving in her right hand.

Then it happened.

She advanced suddenly yet methodically, standing in front of him with her back toward me. It was almost as if she planned to block my view and provide the security of the secrecy she thrived on.

All I could see was the fear in David's face and the pain in his eyes as he bent over. He was holding his chest with both hands and blood seeped between his fingers. I could taste the adrenaline that now flowed throughout my body. The fear and horror that I felt were nothing compared to the sheer terror I saw in his eyes.

"You stabbed him! You stabbed him! You stabbed him!" I repeated in horror.

Her face suddenly became clear and emotionless. She ignored my screams and coldly took David by the arm and led him to the bathroom. I followed them, and I was terrified to see her slowly separating his bleeding flesh with her fingers to determine the depth of the cut, and then stuffing some old dirty cloth in the wound. Her actions were mechanical. She was able to suppress all emotion as she went about the next few minutes.

"You killed him! You killed him! You killed him!" I repeated over and over, scared out of my mind.

I knew what she had done and yet I couldn't believe that she'd actually done it. I was petrified. I didn't know it was possible. I just couldn't believe that she could do it—kill someone. I mean kill her son, even if it was only IT. I was always afraid that she would someday kill, but now I believed she actually had done it.

She suddenly stopped. Completely devoid of emotion, she ordered me out of the room. I ran to my bedroom, I ran from her. I ran for my life. She now had the power to kill. As ashamed as I am to admit it, I was more fearful that she might kill me than of the possibility of my brother bleeding to death in the bathroom.

For days afterward I'd see David leaning up against the base of the washing machine in the dark basement. He was cringing in pain and shivering as he swabbed away the seepage that oozed from the sliced flesh of his chest.

For the first time I really felt that he needed help. For a brief moment the thought of seeking help for him from the outside world came into my mind. I knew in my heart that he was dying—and yet the fear of his departure only meant the reality of my arrival.

I wanted him to live.

I needed him to live.

The fear of him dying was more than just losing a brother. I needed him to live so I wouldn't be the one lying on the cold damp cement wondering if I was going to live through the night.

It was a matter of survival.

Deep down I knew that the gates of Hell would open and I would receive far more than I had ever gotten in the past if I opened my mouth to anyone about what Mom was doing. I was a coward and for the first time I knew why my father just stood there when he was living with us. He, too, was afraid. Dad was six foot something and 250 pounds of solid man, and he, too, was afraid—afraid of his wife.

Over the next few days I would spy on David as he cleaned out his wound as best he could. He endured the pain from the infection. There was no medical care, and no one outside the house knew just what happened in the kitchen that night.

Soon things were getting back to normal—for us, anyway. David was able to methodically respond as before. Mom never changed pace or showed any sorrow over the near killing of one of her own children. She had now shown that she was not only capable of killing, but also willing to do so. I could tell that Mom was becoming something different, or perhaps I was just now at the tender age of seven, becoming more aware of just who she really was.

She was becoming more open in her treatment of my brother. My understanding was becoming clearer. I started to realize that she had been preparing herself to kill David for years. I learned from that petrifying experience in the kitchen that Mom was capable of far more than I had ever thought. I was scared to be near her and would rather have faced the monster at the bottom of the steps than face her alone and me trapped in some corner of the basement.

―――――――

The last memories I have of David after the kitchen accident were not long after Christmas 1972. I was eight years old at the time, and for some reason Mom had suddenly insisted that my younger brother, Keith, and I stay at Uncle Dennis and Aunt Jessica's house in San Francisco for several days. Ross and Scott had been mysteriously quiet and secretive about the whole thing, refusing to answer my questions. They were afraid to tell me at the time, but I later learned what they were doing.

"Why are we staying there? What are you guys doing without us?" I asked.

The fact that we were even staying with Uncle Dennis was extremely strange. I knew that Mom loathed her brother. She hated anyone who stood up to her. Uncle Dennis was the only one who would tell her off over the phone about how she disciplined her children. So the contact she had with him had been a complete surprise to me. There had to be a reason that she allowed us to spend time there without her being at my side to monitor what I said or did.

Uncle Dennis was a stern man and was fond of hunting. In the front room he had a chair that was just his; no one could sit in it without his permission. Off to the left of the chair was a small table made out of a tree stump polished and lacquered. On the wall were brass ducks flying together. He loved ducks. They were a predominant theme throughout his house. He showed me how to pluck feathers off ducks that he had recently shot. I kept the feathers a secret and stored them in a small plastic bag. I felt that this was such an odd situation—staying at Mom's brother's house in secrecy. I thought that if I had any evidence that I had been at Uncle Dennis's house, Mom would get angry with me and hurt me. I had to keep the feathers a secret from the whole world. I wasn't sure who wasn't supposed to know where I had been for those few days.

There had to be a reason, I just had no idea at the time what was really going on. All I knew was that I was afraid. I was afraid of what I wasn't being told. And then I thought about the knife.

Did she finally do it? Did she actually kill IT? Or did she kill someone else? I wondered secretly and in fear.

All the time I spent at my uncle's house I kept wondering what was happening back home. I looked to my older cousin for comfort and yet I didn't know if he was aware of what was happening to us. I wanted to ask him for help and yet I was afraid to. I just didn't know what to do. I was away from my familiar surroundings and was kept in the dark while I was there. My cousins didn't seem too concerned about the situation and why we were staying there day after day.

Sean, my oldest cousin, was at least ten or twelve years older than me. He had a pool table in the basement of his home, and allowed me to shoot pool as if I knew how to play the game. Much like my own brother Ross, my cousin Sean was kind to and tolerant of me and my younger brother, now nearly three.

Each day Mom would pick us up late in the evening and return us early each morning. This went on for four or five days.

The last day we were taken to Uncle Dennis's, Mom had gotten up early, showered, and done her hair. She was wearing a black dress that fit neatly. She looked like a different person. She looked presentable and even happy, like she was in those old photos. The vague hope that she had returned to the normal person she must have once been passed through my mind.

As she dropped us off, I mustered up the courage to finally ask her, "Why are we staying here? What's happening to us?"

All she said was: "Just listen to Uncle Dennis and stay out of trouble! The future of my family depends on it."

I had heard her use the term *my family* often whenever she needed to separate me from the rest of the boys, but this time she meant it. Before this moment, I had always been her informer as far as my brother was concerned and more or less part of her family. Mom had successfully allowed me to feel safe when I was turning over on my own brother. Now she was deliberately and carefully making me feel excluded; making me feel like David must have felt—separated and singled out. I wasn't sure if my thoughts of David leaving were becoming a reality and I was now moving into his place. I started to wonder if Mom wanted to treat me the same way she had treated David. Deep down inside, I desperately tried to convince myself that I was not becoming his replacement.

The last day she picked up my brother and me from Uncle Dennis's, I expected some explanation of what had happened, the reason we were excluded from knowing what went on. But as usual, she let me know nothing.

She acted as if nothing had happened, and she made sure life returned to the same routines of her heavy drinking and staying up late at night walking the house by herself.

Within a day or so of returning home, I overheard my older brothers discussing the fact that IT was no longer at the house.

When I first heard the news I knew I was right—Mom had finally killed him. She must have been pushed too far. Or perhaps he had failed once again to perform his duties the night before. I was horrified by that thought, and yet it somehow didn't seem all that strange. It was as if I had been expecting it all my life. As sad as it is to say, I really expected David to die.

The thought of his murder terrified me. I couldn't bring myself to accept the possibility of her going through with it. I just refused to accept the idea that she had finally killed him. I knew that she was capable of killing but I'd held on to the hope that she would never be able to actually do it.

It was the next afternoon that she told me that he wasn't dead.

"The police have taken him away!" she proudly announced.

Mom made sure it was clear to me that his disloyalty and his disobedience had caused the police to take him to some sort of child jail and how miserable he must now be.

That night, as I lay in bed reliving my memories of him and trying to cope with my guilt, a feeling of uncertainty and fear started to grow in my heart. It was as if my recurring nightmare was now coming true, and I was sliding down the stairs toward the monster that would inevitably swallow my soul. Suddenly I thought of the basement and of the green army cot, and the childish envy I had once felt for not being able to sleep there seemed terribly stupid.

As the hours passed, I grew more and more scared. I prayed to God that he would forgive me and keep me from falling into David's place. I begged in prayer.

Finally I understood. If there was a God, surely he would never have allowed any of this to happen to David or me.

So once again, I was left alone.

Now I was aware of what she was capable of and just how far she would go. She had crossed over that fine line, and I was sure I was her next victim.

4

NO ONE

The wishes and beliefs of childhood are among the strongest emotions we'll experience. For me, I wished and hoped that someone would step in and help me. At the time I didn't realize it, but the authorities were well aware of what Mom was doing, and yet nothing ever occurred that would have stopped her. No one did anything.

Now my life was making more sense. I'd never really thought about it before David left, but I began to realize that I was never treated exactly like he was. Mom and I had our own fights. We had always had our own arguments. I would get hit or knocked down as punishment for something I knew nothing about. That's just the way it was. I never sat down and thought about the difference between David and me before. I always knew that I didn't want to "be" him. I didn't want to experience his dreadful plight.

I was never a favorite of Mom's. When it came to her showing support and confidence in her kids, she always excluded me. She never hesitated to support Ross and Scott.

The one thing that made me different than the rest was—I was Mom's confidant, no one else. I was comfortable in bringing out flaws in anyone else to Mom just to hide my own shortcomings. I knew that if I kept Mom close to me in that respect, it meant she was after someone else and not me. That's all I really wanted.

When David was there, Mom would always rather beat him than yell at me. Although she made me feel small and ugly, she never treated me as she did David. She never actually tried to kill me. I guess I had it pretty good. But now he was gone and Mom was still the same—crazy.

Apparently, as Mom had said, the police had taken David away while my younger brother and I were at Uncle Dennis's house in San Francisco. I was told that he was a criminal, and I was shocked when Mom told me he had attempted to burn down the school. Also, she said, he had stolen food from other children, he had lied, and he had committed unspeakable acts of violence against other students and even teachers. With each passing day after his disappearance, the stories Mom told me seemed to grow, the stories of the misdeeds this child had committed. How he could have done such things was beyond me. I must admit I felt a certain jealousy that someone like him could live such an adventurous life while mine was so insignificant. I didn't know what to think. I was learning that he had the same capabilities that I'd recently seen in Mom. I was now scared of him. I never imagined that poor David could be that cruel and evil.

Yet in truth I felt incredibly sad. Deep inside I knew that I had caused him great harm, and I knew he hated me for it. Now I would never be able to make up for what I had done. I would never be able to tell him that, in spite of it all, I loved him with a brotherly love I was never allowed to show. All of us were scared of Mom in some way or another. I think Ross and Scott were scared from what they saw IT go through. I don't recall them ever getting any beatings like he got.

I made my way into the kitchen to look for some bread to toast or some cereal for breakfast. I felt a sense of emptiness as I strained to listen for the cries and the slaps that used to echo up the staircase, expecting to deliberately tune them out as I always did, but there was only silence.

Stepping into the kitchen, I suddenly remembered how Dad had made me toast for breakfast one morning. I just knew that when he was around, it was a special occasion and usually didn't last long. When he left, I felt abandoned. Just like David, he was gone, and I was still there.

As I stood in the kitchen I recalled how Dad would sit in the recliner in the corner of the living room next to the large bay window that overlooked the bay and the Golden Gate Bridge. He would respond to Mom's description of what "the Boy" did today by simply mumbling back at her.

"Let the Boy eat, he needs to eat something," he would say in anger.

I never really thought about it, but I guess Dad had accepted the way his wife had been treating his kids and accepted that fact that he couldn't or wouldn't do anything about it. Perhaps he truly was afraid of her, too.

He'd hold his paper high enough to cover his face; all I could hear was Dad exclaiming, "the Boy this," and "the Boy that."

Even Dad forgot his name.

As I started to think about Dad, I realized that he was the guy I was supposed to hate, the man that I was instructed by Mom to remember as a coward. That's how she talked about him, always in the past tense and always in anger. Since I was always expected to agree with Mom and follow her feelings as if they were my own, I hated him, too. I didn't know why I hated him. I was told to and I never questioned it. I was afraid to.

"He doesn't deserve the family values we have in this house!" Mom would often say.

———————

I place my breakfast on a plate, leave it on the dining room table, leave the plate, and walk to the bedroom. I feel sadness as I look at the clothes that I'm so tired of. I'm constantly getting laughed at over them. The red corduroy pants and the green short-sleeved shirt are clothes that I've worn a hundred times this year alone. Today they're especially dirty from playing with my Matchbox cars in the backyard on the hill the day before. I can't recall now why I didn't have time to wash them. I pull the shirt over my head and my pants up and leave the room.

By now my two older brothers Ross and Scott are all sitting at the dining room table. Ross has his breakfast of poached eggs on toast and juice, lovingly made by the gentle hands of "Mother." A little more pepper than I think I would like. Then again, I can only imagine that I could have such a breakfast. Scott doesn't get the eggs and toast; he gets whatever he wants. Scott can ask and she responds without hesitation. I have to make whatever I can for breakfast and only when I can. Sometimes I have to skip breakfast and start running away from her and try to get out the door once I'm dressed. Since David left, she's started slapping me in the morning more and more.

I let my mind wander as I sit at the table. I get confused when I try to recall how things were before David left us. I know that he was the only one who was forced to eat under the kitchen table when the rest of the family ate at the dining room table.

I begin to understand that there are some things that haven't changed and some things that have. Now I'm never able to do anything without her permission. I can't eat dinner, I can't take a bath, I can't do a thing without her knowing. As I think about it, I begin to recognize a few changes around the house that maybe I had overlooked before.

Lately when dinner is served I have to wait until Keith is served and has started to eat his meal before I can pick up a fork.

"Keith isn't ready yet. You can wait!" she shouts.

I never question what she says. I never question anything. Mom thinks I'm done with my dinner whenever Keith is done with his. Keith finishes and she simply removes his plate and my own at the same time.

I understand that I have to eat faster, and can start only after Keith has begun. The other boys go about their dinner as usual. Most of the time, I think I'm in trouble for something I've done wrong, but she never tells me what it is and I'm too afraid to ask.

As I think about how things have changed, I begin to wonder what she is up to. Mom has wasted no time in making me feel like he must have felt.

Mom has no one like David around to beat on anymore. I am more afraid of her than ever. I get in more trouble for anything I do or say. Now I find that I'm always in trouble and I don't know why. Now that David is gone, I'm afraid that she will try to kill me, like she tried to kill him. I'm afraid that she will treat me like an animal, like she did him. I'm afraid that now I'm her IT.

As I watch Mom in the kitchen, I see how she takes such good care of the other boys. For Ross, she makes sure that breakfast is just right. I see her in the kitchen, the floor speckled with the black, orange, and green shapes so common in the 1970s. I can see the white metal table, the white cabinets, and the olive-green stove as she goes about her business.

For a moment I imagine her preparing something just for me.

I would be a better boy if I thought she liked me as much as Ross or Scott.

They have clean clothes. Ross has book covers bought at school that carefully protect his books. The ones I have are made of paper bags I cut out and attempt to make fit. I can't ever get it right. Any kid could tell that an eight-year-old made them.

I'm quickly brought back to reality as she comes to the table, snatches away my plate of toast, and informs me that I'm done with breakfast. She moves into the dining room, takes the plate, and walks back into the kitchen as she talks to herself, never missing a step. As I sit there, Ross eats his breakfast and drinks his juice. Sometimes I get mad at him because he is the biggest and he never stands up to her. Even though he is only a boy himself, if anyone is going to stand up for me, he should.

Why do you just sit there? I ponder in anger. I want to scream at him and force him to wake up and see what's going on.

Stand up to her! Do something!

The more I think about what I wish I could say out loud, the angrier I get.

I look at him as he carefully glances over at me and ensures that Mom can't see him. He slides one of the grape-jelly pieces of toast over to me and I pull it under the table and out of sight. His silent smile reassures me that he understands and cares.

All is forgiven. I feel safe with him, and the hunger doesn't matter. My ill feelings are replaced with a sense of fullness, as if I have eaten all I possibly can. I smile back at him and she walks in. The two of us return to normal before she even knows what happened. All it takes for me to forget my anger is a simple piece of bread and a small smile. We are friends, we are brothers.

I leave the table and begin my morning ritual of running around the house trying to get away from her before school starts. I have always had to run from Mom in the morning. It's like some cruel game. I know it and she knows it. We both know that I run from her and try to miss being spanked or slapped before school. We both know that the other is aware of this ugly game.

"Why do you always have to run around and start something?" Scott always asks. It's the one thing I can count on from Scott. He knows full well what is going on. He pretends to not know or not understand. He is doing what I once did to be on Mom's side.

"All I did was wake up," I say angrily under my breath.

———————

Finally getting away from her, I go to my room and look at all the furniture and the old pieces of junk I've been collecting. They are obstacles placed strategically throughout the room to provide time when I need to get away from her. Looking at the obstacle path, I can't stop thinking. Something has changed in the house, but I don't know what, something about Mom.

If Mom really wants to get me when I run away from her, why doesn't she just throw all this furniture out when I'm at school? She could easily take my one and only security away from me, but she doesn't.

As I look at the furniture around my room I see all the items discarded by the neighbors. I take only the ones that will provide safety when carefully placed in my room. I know that she can't catch me if I'm on one side of the pile of furniture and she is on the other.

As I go through my day, I always look for anything that can be used. The thought that they need to work or look good doesn't matter to me. I need them for protection.

They have one job, to keep her away. A pine boomerang-shaped table and a broken black lacquer-and-glass stereo cabinet are in the center of my collection. A couple of end tables painted bright orange are scattered in the center of the pile. Carefully placed on the outside of the pile is a medium-sized TV stand made from pale yellow Formica with silver metal edges. It serves as the last place to jump into and hide when I can't get away from Mom any other way. I have been saving it because it makes me feel safe knowing that it is there if I need it.

Mom always catches me before I leave the house for the walk to school. I walk the obstacle course in my room to see if there is anything in the way, such as shoes on the floor that I could trip over, or something out of place. Walking around the maze of things I have collected to ensure that all is right, I'm comfortable. Everything is in its place.

Sometimes I get angry with my brothers for not helping me. They know that she chases me around each morning and most nights as she tries to hit me for something. They complain about the noise I make and how I interrupt their television as I run in front of it trying to keep her away from me. It's as if they accept it and just sort of tune me out.

They're tuning me out, just like I did to—him.

She never had to constantly beat me, only occasionally, to keep me frightened of her, and she knew that. All she had to

enough for me that she knew. Her touch was soft and she rubbed my hair when I walked into their house looking for Josh to play with. This let me know that at least she was concerned. We both wanted to say what we knew was the truth, yet neither of us had the guts to open our mouths.

Susan started a signaling system that would inform me when Josh was ready to leave the house. Once Josh was ready, Susan would open the front blinds of their house. This would let me know that I should be on my way out the front door. We created this system after Josh confessed to me that he wasn't comfortable coming over or into my house anymore. My best friend was just as scared of my mom as I was. He was told by his parents to stay away.

I was crushed. My best friend had now pulled away from me because there were many things that were changing. Initially they were little changes, and so many that it felt as though they'd crept up slowly. Between the way the neighbors looked at me and the teachers always watched me and talked about me to one another, it was embarrassing. It wasn't as if all at once my best friend and his family started to treat me differently. But when the neighbors realized one of the boys was missing, I began to realize that a lot had changed.

"The police took him away," I would repeat over and over to anyone who dared to ask.

It was the standard answer to questions that other people asked. Such as Josh's parents. No one really wanted to get to the bottom of the disappearance of an eleven-year-old boy named David. All those neighbors, students, classmates, and even a few of the teachers knew he had been taken away. No one ever asked why. They all knew why. They just never spoke about it. Like me, they were afraid to.

It was hard to accept that my best friend's loyalty was changing right before my eyes. He started to act differently toward me, as if he was scared of me, or scared of something.

I sat on the desk at the base of the windows in my room, waiting for the signal from across the street. I daydreamed of Josh and his house.

Does Susan make them breakfast?

Do they have to run from their mom?

Mom has managed to sneak into the room without me noticing. I've trained so hard and long to be completely aware of her whenever she tries to sneak up and grab me by the arm or leg. I usually run away before she can start hitting me.

She tells me, as she reaches for my arms, that Susan has opened the front blinds. Susan is now watching from her front door to make sure that Josh and I both make it out of our houses.

Now I must stand up and run. I've been sitting on a desk looking at Josh's house and didn't notice the blinds. As I jump to the floor I slip on the hardwood covered by the dust that has been accumulating for weeks, since I last swept the floor. Mom reaches out for me on the floor with her claws to grab me, but doesn't grab me tight enough.

Instant fear and panic set in. I squirm and break free from her grip. Up and on I go, around the center of the room, around and around with Mom right behind me. I run past the corner of the boomerang-shaped table and the nightstand in front of the desk. There's only two feet between the bed and the table's corner, just enough room for me to turn the corner and keep running. Just past the bed sits the old stereo cabinet and I make it past another corner. This time there's only a foot or so between the cabinet and the closet doors— just enough room for me to run between them. The pounding in my chest helps me focus on running away from her and makes me run faster.

Mom shouts out some swear word at me as she pushes the cabinet out of the way to continue chasing me. The whole room is only about one hundred fifty square feet and nearly all of that is made up of the junk I've collected, which has now proven itself valuable once again. I keep my silence as I run. I know from past experiences that if I yell for help or cry out for fear, she will get angrier.

Down the hall, I pass her room, then the bathroom, and race into the kitchen. Faster and faster I go. I feel confident this morning and recall how Ross made me feel at breakfast, proud and comfortable. I make it to the dining room table, hoping to slide under it to get on the other side before she catches me. But I can tell I'm losing the race. As I carefully dive under the table to the other side, I bang my knee on the leg of one of the chairs tucked under the table. The table is old and heavy, made of solid wood with one armchair at each end. The fancy carvings on the legs of the table and chairs show the marks we have made and tell stories of mornings just like this one. The massive legs are marked with the scratchings and clawings of countless animals and kids. Years of scars are visible, evident in the dark wood.

I get up and try to run as fast as I can to the living room. My heart is pounding faster and faster, and the fear becomes panic. As I look back, I can't see her. Suddenly she grabs my arm. In one hand she has a firm grip on my arm and in her other hand, a chair from the kitchen. She carefully places the chair in the front room directly across from the front door. I have no idea what godforsaken plot she has cooked up today. I squirm, begging her to let go.

"I didn't do anything!" I cry out.

I don't know how much time has passed. Josh, who was waiting in the front yard, has now come up to the front door. I hear the doorbell and scream.

"No!" I cry out.

Now I realize what she has selected for my kiss good-bye. I am crushed with disappointment and filled with embarrassment. She continues to hold my arm tighter and tighter. As I'm squirming away, I can tell what's going to happen next. Panic becomes terror. She opens the door and Josh asks if I'm ready for school, never looking at her. He's just looking at me standing off balance, leaning away from her as she holds on to my arm that is now turning red from her grip.

"Just a minute, honey!" Mom politely tells Josh.

As if she is Wally Cleaver's mother, reaching for the child's lunch bag she has just made with love, she pulls my dirty green shirt over my head, but not off my body. It catches on my arms. Unable to reach anything or even know what direction I have been spun in, she rips my pants down and exposes my briefs to Josh. I nearly die of embarrassment and I'm again speechless.

She sits down and throws me across her lap and starts spanking me. Blow after blow she continues, never saying a word, harder and harder as she develops a good rhythm. I swear she is singing softly to herself as she spanks me, and is unaware of the terror in Josh's eyes, or of my cries. Finally Josh says he has to go now or he will be late for school, in a voice loud enough to be heard over the spanks and runs down the front steps. With that she lets me go and I fall to the floor. Unable to see with my shirt and arms still over my head, I try to pull up my pants up as I go out the door.

Once again, Josh has waited for me and never says a word about what he sees in the house. Maybe that is why we are such good friends. We always find another topic to talk about on the walk to school, anything at all, anything except what just happened.

The walk today is especially hard as the cotton material of my briefs is rubbing against the tender skin that was so red a few minutes ago. Today it's very bad. I try to hold back the tears and my eyes fill up as I recall the fear on Josh's face. I am crying for what Josh saw and how he will grow farther and farther from me. I am crying for the disappointment I had in myself for not being prepared and breaking free from her grip, and I am crying for the heartache I know all too well.

Josh and I have found out a special path from our houses to the school. We walk down the end of Crestline Avenue to

Westmore Avenue, then down Edgemont Drive past West-more Park. Along the edge of Westmore Park is a grove of trees with an obvious path through, cut out by hundreds of kids walking the same trail. The trees provide great cover as we yell and run faster and faster along our way.

Today is different, and I tell Josh that I can't walk anymore. I need to rest awhile. He agrees and goes on to tell my teacher that I am running late again. He is always good about that. He's not very imaginative about new excuses, but very loyal.

There is a place near the far end of the Westmore High football field that borders the grove of trees. I often go there and lie on my back. Today I'm unable to dream of what things should be like. I know I daydream too much, but I have nothing else, just my short dreams of freedom, dreams of *The Brady Bunch.*

How can any family be that happy?

Without warning I catch myself.

I jump up and shout at the top of my voice: "I'm just a kid—leave me alone!"

I don't know to whom I'm crying out, God maybe. That invisible person who is supposed to be there when you call, the last hope of help and true love. He never responds to my cries, aloud or silent. God becomes only a name, a title. Perhaps I'm shouting at Mom, or myself.

I must deserve this treatment, since no one stops it from happening. Not Josh's parents, who told me they knew what was happening. Not the school where I'm constantly called down to the office for questions about my home situation. They tell me "we're aware of the situation." Not my brothers, who now just tune me out as Mom chases me and ends up slapping or kicking me for nothing more than simply being alive. Unexpectedly, I welcome the surfacing anger at my father that I seldom find. Anger that he left us. Anger that he left me, anger at his freedom from Mom.

I want a normal life and a father who works hard and comes home to the family, a mother who cares for the family's needs and provides the necessary things in life with love and concern. I must really be a bad kid to have this life; I must deserve it.

They must all be right: My feelings of being worthless and undeserving of life itself are true.

Another day of convincing myself that I am what I'm told I am, and after a short while I'm up and on my way to school.

Mom had always said that the police took David away, and although that had some truth to it, it wasn't anything like the stories Mom had told me. I wasn't aware of it at the time, but the reality of it was that the school started the whole process of removing him from the house. They were the ones who finally stood up and said, *Enough is enough.*

Since I had no idea of that reality at the time, I had little faith in the numerous trips I was required to take down to the principal's office. If I had been given the slightest clue that they really did care, and that they had the power to help, I would have told them everything. Since they already had the police and the state social services involved, I should have been able to expect help, but it never came.

The state, in all its wisdom, took only one of the five boys from the home. To this day, some thirty years later, I have no idea why only one boy was taken. Did they really think that a parent who was cruel and evil, one who has tried multiple times to kill her own kids, would select only one child to abuse? Did they think that someone so twisted and sick would be able to stop the lifestyle of abuse and mayhem? They took only one and left the rest of us to suffer.

The elementary school was about a forty-five-minute walk from the house and was divided into wings. Each wing was dedicated to certain grades. The kindergarten area was closest to the office and library. The first and second grades had the next wing, and so on. The last wing was made up of the older kids, who were in fifth and sixth grades.

The playground was as large as the school. Although it wasn't actually divided into sections, it was obvious to anyone that the grades were divided in the play area as well. The swing sets and the slides were closest to the first-grade area; the basketball courts were farthest away from the younger kids' play area.

In kindergarten I played with wooden blocks and willingly gave them up when another kid challenged me for them. I just couldn't find the courage to fight back, or stand up for myself. That was just the beginning of behavior that followed me throughout all of my school years. Although the classes were fairly small, maybe twenty kids, the other kids knew each other. As we moved up from grade to grade, we all knew who was trouble, who was cruel, and who got picked on.

By the time I was in second grade, and David had just been taken away, I was already labeled as an easy target. I guess it was from my ability to hold my emotions inside and simply take whatever was handed out to me. Cruelty and physical and verbal abuse was simply part of my life at home, so why should school have been any different? I felt small and ashamed.

When I turned eight, things really started to get bad for me in school. Most of us walked to school, and I would see the same faces of the children as they left their houses and walked the same paths to the school as Josh and I did. It wasn't long before the walk became so routine that I could tell if I was running late or not by whether I missed seeing some of the kids walking out of their homes when Josh and I passed by.

The last part of the walk included crossing the street at the firehouse on the corner and then walking into the schoolyard and along the fence to the grassy area at the back of the school grounds. As the fence ended, the grassy area began. That was where the "attack" usually happened. Every time I approached that portion of fence my heart would race and my palms would sweat. I was so scared of that part of the walk.

Three particular kids at the school knew the route I took to school each morning and also knew I was an easy target. They waited for me at the end of the fence and sprang out of the bushes to torment me. Usually they left Josh alone. He would watch as they made their remarks and laughed and made fun of my clothes and the fact that I had red hair and freckles. On the few occasions that Josh left me with them—because they had kept us there for so long—I felt disappointed that he would abandon me. He might as well have been in Switzerland, he was so far away from standing up for me.

The torment would usually end with a quick shove into the bushes. I could hear their laughter as they ran into the schoolyard and left me. Most of the time my pants were already muddy and dirty anyway, so the mud that I wiped off as I stood up from the bushes didn't really matter to me. Even as I stood in line each morning to get my lunch ticket, kids would stand in groups and mock the little boy in filthy clothes. I was angry and embarrassed at the same time.

"He's worn the same pants all year long."

"He can't afford any clothes."

"His mother is a boozer!" the kids used to say. The fact that they nailed Mom wasn't upsetting to me. I really didn't care about her. It was my embarrassment over the clothes I had at the time that really hurt.

The early bell rings. It is the one that signals the start of the school day, but I am already dreading the walk home. The amount of harassment I get from the other kids has been low today, as it is clear that something is wrong with me. I must look even worse than usual. My pride is gone. I have no desire to pay any attention or even try to look interested. I'm now more comfortable laying my head on the desk and trying to sleep. It's hard to keep still. The cotton material of my underwear sticks to my skin as the blood dries from this morning's harsh spanking. Once again I'm called down to the principal's office. For the last several weeks I have been called down almost daily. Ever since David left all I hear is that I'm the one that they are concerned about. I'm sure they believe, just like Mom does, that I'm no good and I need to be watched. They, too, must know that I'm always getting in trouble for something. Perhaps Mom has told them lies about me as she lied about David.

Once I'm in the office the conversation is short, with me mostly just listening but not paying attention to what is said. Within a few minutes I'm back on my way to the classroom.

Down the hall from the office is the library—the one place I love to go. I can find a book and sit in a corner, all alone in the new world I find between the covers. I always find books about adventure or books about space and my favorite animals. Today I slip in unnoticed, as a class is already in the library. Off in the corner, I start looking for titles that catch my eye. Eventually finding one, I scan the room for a place to sit in the sunlight. Once again I find my favorite spot open— near the tall glass windows where the morning sun heats the surroundings. But it doesn't take long before the pain reminds me that today, sitting isn't going to happen. Frustrated that she can affect me even when she's not around, I throw the book on the floor and run out unnoticed.

As I walk back to the classroom I detour into the boys' room. I find an open stall, lock myself in, and cry. I often spend a lot of time in there just crying, never loud enough for anyone to hear. I sit there for a long time with my empty cries to God for help. The last class of the day is about to start. By the sound of the bell, I know that kids will be coming into the boys' room soon and I must get out before they see me. The embarrassment would be too much if they saw me crying. It would just give the boys who harass me another reason to do it again. The entire day has passed me by and I have barely been in the classroom. Between the principal's office and my lazy walks back to class, I've managed to waste the day. It never matters to me—no one ever misses me.

As I wipe my eyes on my sleeve, I can tell that it has left more dirt on my face than was there before. Now I have to wash. I can see my reflection in the water as I fill the sink. When I look into the mirror I feel the same disgust and shame that I always see in myself: the screaming red hair, uncombed, and the dirty face. I hang my head in shame.

Why are you here?

Why don't you just finish it?

I know I would never have the guts to actually take my own life, so the desire becomes only a dream. Strangely enough, that dream of one day taking my own life gives me a sense of comfort.

I walk slowly out of the orange doors and into the courtyard with not a kid in sight. As I walk straight ahead, the silence of the massive courtyard and the silence in my head allow me to hear the blood flow through my ears. With my head hung low, I can see the gravel packed into the blacktop courtyard. Walking and thinking, I reach the end of the pavement. There the lawn begins for the ball field and the play area for the older kids in school. Seeing nobody, I lie on my back and wonder again: *Should I?*

I stand up and decide to walk back to what is left of school today. Before I can make it back to the hallway, the last bell of the day rings and the halls fill with the sounds of kids closing their lockers.

I look for Josh in the middle of the large playground area in the rear of the school. This is one of two meeting places we have. There is no sign of my friend. Walking back through the halls and along the path near the library that leads into the parking lot, I find him in the second meeting spot, near the end of the hallway. I smile when I see him and he waves me over to where he stands. We step together as we walk silently. Josh knows that I get harassed over my clothes and my constant smell of dirt and sweat. Again, not a word is said. Both Josh and I know that we can rely on each other for friendship. He has seen me at my worst and I have listened as he expresses his frustration with being the oldest and having a younger brother and sister.

Nearing the top of the long street that leads to the top of Westmore Hill, I can't keep up with Josh, and I ask that we stop in the trees and just look around.

"I can't today. I have to go with my mom out shopping for clothes for school pictures," he proudly calls back to me.

I try not to show my jealousy and anger. First off, I forgot that school pictures were next week. More important, I forgot that I would have to stand in line behind all the kids in their new clothes and I still would be in my old rags, smelling of sweat and dirt. The embarrassment is just too much.

Once Josh is out of sight, I turn and run into the woods, crying. I'm so mad at the thought of him in new clothes and me in the same old red pants and green shirt. I stop, lie on my back, and look up at the blue sky dotted with the few white clouds that slowly pass overhead.

"So, God—where were you today?" I ask in anger.

I got up and on my way to the place called "Home." Turning the corner at the bottom of Crestline Avenue, I could see the house and the dismal colors that in my mind set it apart from the others on the street. In reality, the house was painted pink and was just as bright as the rest of the houses in the neighborhood. I was desperate for the miracle of natural disaster. If only a hurricane, tornado, or earthquake would take that one house. I was angry to find it still standing there.

I don't recall what we fought about when I got home. I know that she chased me around the house before dinner. Right after dinner I simply went to bed, tired from the day, tired from the evening, and tired of life itself.

That night I followed the same plan of pretending to be asleep. I remember so clearly that it was this particular night that I decided I must try to sleep with my eyes open, sleeping while still being able to see any movement. That way I could fool even her. I was sure I was the next one in line. Taking David's place, the routine, and the shame he must have felt, was just too much for me to deal with.

I thought of David's leaving and more anger built up inside me. He actually left me without saying good-bye. Perhaps he didn't want to. Perhaps he hated me for the things I blamed on him and the beatings he took for it. Perhaps he was truly angry and had no desire to show any emotion or concern for those he left behind—the other children, or that house.

I was confused; I couldn't tell if I should be angry that he'd left me behind to become his replacement or happy for him for getting out. I hadn't thought too much about what he was now going through. All I knew was that he was free and I was not. I was left behind. I was forgotten. Deep down I knew that he had no intention of helping me. *Why should he?* I thought.

At the age of eight, I learned what it meant to be betrayed. It took me more than twenty years to learn the truth. The fact was, he couldn't have helped me. He was just a boy himself, and he was starting over. He had his freedom and he was entitled to it. Had I had the same chance—I don't know what I would have done.

6

THE BREAK

At the age of nine I had become so timid and afraid of everything that I seldom looked any farther than my own little corner of the world and my bedroom for anything or anybody. I had become just what Mom wanted: an obedient punching bag. But for the first time ever, I found enough courage to at least try to run away and leave her forever. Unfortunately, as a child I knew I just couldn't stand up to her. I didn't have the resolve to make a stand.

MOM OFTEN REMINDED ME that I should consider myself lucky, that I really wasn't in such a bad place. This advice was supposed to give me a reason to stick with following Mom's wishes and not fighting back.

But David was gone. He was the one who got away! He was the one who broke the chains of Hell. Even if he was in a prison, what better place to be? Even when he was supposed to be gone from my mind, he never was. I could sit and imagine him alone and crying in some dark cell. That was all I could imagine. I had no idea of the real life he was just starting for himself.

School vacation was nearing its end, and the days started getting shorter as fall approached. Signs of seasonal changes gave my otherwise miserable life direction. The most important signal was the streetlights turning on at dusk, indicating that we had only half an hour left to play in the street. There was little traffic on Crestline Avenue. Playing in the street was common, not just for us, but for most of the kids our age. Although Mom found it necessary to watch every move I made, she was careful to allow some appearance of normalcy to exist. Just to fool the neighbors. She wouldn't allow me to talk to her unless I was spoken to, lift my head up from my chest and look at her unless I was told to, or even get out of bed without her permission. The other boys, my brothers, those who were left, could speak freely and say whatever was on their minds.

Playing outside was a joy for me. I could run and play and speak without fear. Within a few moments of being allowed to go to the front yard, I felt a sense of joy. Speaking to Josh or my brothers without stuttering or being mimicked reminded me just how frightened I was of Mom. Outside the house I was comfortable.

My oldest brother, Ross, would often play a sort of football game with Josh and me. We would ride our bikes as Ross would throw the football and see if he could hit us as moving targets. It never actually hurt. After all, he was my brother. I enjoyed being with him more than anything in the world. I would have taken a hundred falls off the bike just to play and be near him. Even though he had better things to do, he would still play with me. When his older friends came by, he would never prevent me from spending time with him. He and I were friends, both of us knowing, but neither of us willing to discuss, our life. *Afraid to talk about it* is probably closer to the truth.

My brother Scott and I were completely different. His relationship with Mom was one of companionship and trust, almost as if he took Dad's place. They often discussed punishments for me as if I weren't even in the room. He was able to find trust and confidence from her that I could only recall when I was Mom's Little Nazi. The relationship he and I had was one of competition and jealousy, always trying to outdo each other. As weird as it is, in a way it was justice: Scott was now in the place where I once was.

Scott's place in the family became special. He was singled out as "off limits," not to be teased or hurt in any way. The consequences for even causing a tear were bad. Eventually he turned this into a kind of power over me. He was able to convince Mom that whatever he said was the absolute truth. He did to me just as I once had done to David. She believed me without hesitation back then just as she now did with Scott.

"It would have been fine if Richard had left it alone!" Scott would often say. I never even knew what the things he was talking about were most of the time. He tinkered with anything from appliances, tools, doors, and walls to small trinkets around the house. I had no interest in anything that wasn't in the middle of my room. I couldn't have cared less about the items that were unfortunate enough to make it to his workshop for repair.

I often thought about Keith and how quiet and comfortable he was. At the age of four, he was good-looking, even cute. Mom always commented on how handsome he was. Since he was so young, Mom spared him any serious harm. He wouldn't have been able to react the same as a seven- or eight-year-old. He wouldn't have shown the fear that Mom craved from a child . . . not at that age, anyway. Keith was like Ross: special, different, yet normal. Normal to Mom, and that's all that mattered. I so wanted to find a way to prevent Keith from becoming the next victim. Thankfully I never had to.

During the summer of 1974 I began to notice certain patterns in Mom that I had overlooked before. Mom had certain habits that were automatic. She would always have a cigarette first thing in the morning. Sit up and light up— first thing in the morning. There were other patterns. She always needed to have her vodka before going to the bathroom after a long night's sleep. I noticed that she was extremely accurate in her times and dates. She could remember the day and hour of anything that I ever did wrong. Of course, she couldn't tell you what day of the week it was if she was asked at any given time, but she seemed to record my life in her head. She had an odd sense of history and how our family was part of history. I can recall her spending months and months working herself into a stupor over our family genealogy. She traced our family history back several generations. There were stories she would tell of the pride and sacrifices made by these ancestors, all for a better life. Discovering new stories and successes of the family, she dug deeper into our past and talked about how she was proud to be a part of that great family.

It was almost as if she thought she was part of the past. In some ways she could lead you to believe that she knew how our ancestors felt or the things they went through. She knew of the harsh and cold winters our forebears experienced as they were scavenging for food and supplies just to survive.

I was intrigued by her animation and her ability to replay these stories in detail. She almost showed a sense of pride in her ability to capture such a fascinating past.

She spoke of the covered wagons, the clothing, the food, and other details—details that only someone who had been there would recall. I believe that she, in some way, actually thought she had been there.

It was afterward that I realized she could carry these stories on for days and days without being abusive. I realized then that she had some sort of mental illness. Her ability to go from one mental state to another in a moment's time and without notice, so smoothly, couldn't possibly have been rehearsed. It was as if she was more than one person.

That summer I started to pay close attention to her changes and see her ability to switch personalities. When she told a story of the old days, she would speak as if she was as old as Grandma while I sat on her knee listening. Next she would be throwing me on the ground and kicking me around for sitting on her knee without asking permission, all in one breath. I began to look for certain movements or a tone of voice that would help me determine who she was. This went on for the entire summer, back and forth from the Mom that I knew to the Mom I wished I had had all along. Many things that summer were new to me.

With each summer there was one sure thing: new clothes. Each year each of the boys would receive a supply of clothes, kept in the dresser in a closet that contained what seemed like tons of clothes for all of us. They were rationed out to each of us as if they were precious. It was several years later that I discovered they were from Grandma in Salt Lake City. Perhaps it was her way of atoning for the sins of her daughter, for knowing full well that her daughter was a drunk, and a violent one at that. She was a drunk who never should have had children. Perhaps it was a way for Grandma to believe that she was, in some way, helping out.

That year I was very excited about getting rid of those old red corduroys and the green short-sleeved shirt I always wore. I was happy to do my chores and finally get the days over with just to be closer to the releasing of the clothes. The days flew by, and the routines became set. I kept quiet out of both love for her and fear of her.

It was almost an unspoken agreement that I would be available for her when she couldn't handle the pressures of life. Whenever she needed to release her twisted anger and violence on one of her own children, I was there.

I found myself accepting my position in the house, and simply planning my life around it as best a ten-year-old could. For instance, I scheduled my turn for laundry after the others had had their clothes washed for them. I'm not sure when, but at one point I was told that since Mom would no longer wash my clothes—she would just wash "the boys' clothes"—I would now be allowed to wash them myself. Prior to this, I wasn't allowed to have clean clothes. She wouldn't wash them, and I wasn't allowed to. I had learned from experience that some clothes shouldn't be washed with others. But I hadn't learned that bleach should be used only on whites. That was one particular error I couldn't hide from Mom. I had ruined my new jeans and changed the color of my T-shirts from white to light blue.

As with anything else, whenever I ruined my clothes by incorrectly washing them, it was taken as a deliberate act of defiance and rebellion. In reality, I simply didn't know how to do it. I was trying to figure it out as I went from day to day. Eventually I was limited to one opportunity a week to do my clothes, since I was taking time away from the other boys, who *needed* their clothes to look clean. I began to believe that I wasn't as smart as my brothers were, or as handsome, and of course not as important. I was reminded from time to time that I was the only one with "those things all over your face and arms," she would say mockingly.

Others called those things "freckles." I admit I looked like Howdy Doody, with screaming red hair, freckles, and a round face. I was unconsciously accepting what was drilled into me. I was different, not as smart, disfigured, and unable to speak. I simply accepted that I was, as she sneered, "disgusting to look at."

Every chance I had to get out of the house, I took. Sometimes that summer I was sent on errands to the local market,

Cala's Market, to buy cigarettes or milk and bread or whatever she required. I remember those long walks to the top of Crestline Avenue and down Eastgate Boulevard, then across the intersection to the market. It took almost an hour but was worth it for the chance to get out. If I was really good or she was in a hurry for something, I could take my bike and ride to the market. I was always being reminded that I shouldn't let anyone see me and I should avoid everyone. Talking to anyone, especially to adults, was absolutely forbidden.

I would make it a point to rush and get there faster than normal so that I had time to walk to the doughnut shop and get a hot chocolate and a doughnut. There was a very nice older woman who seemed to have worked there forever. She knew me as Richard, and knew what to expect when I arrived. She was always well dressed and polite. Her voice was soft and calming. I always felt comfortable whenever I was around her. She made it a point to clear a table near the back of the rows and have me sit there. Perhaps she was worried that my clothes or my appearance would turn customers away, but by giving me a table in the back, she may have been trying to make me more comfortable and less self-conscious. I was often sent on errands directly after one of my mother's explosive beatings. I often looked like hell walking into her store and I knew it.

I was just glad to have someone take care of me, someone whom Mom wasn't aware of. I knew the risk I was taking. I knew that if Mom ever found out I had a friend she couldn't manipulate, she would go crazy.

One day I walked in and was about to ask for my usual hot chocolate when she summoned me over to the end of the rows of tables and sat down with me. She talked about her own kids and how she'd raised them. I was completely absorbed by the stories of kindness and love that were a natural part of her life. She went on for some thirty minutes, with me hanging on every word. The time she spent with her kids doing homework was so foreign to me. I was amazed to think that moms did that. Since I had so few friends, I had no idea what other moms did with their kids. I tried to understand and absorb it all as if it were a foreign language.

I suddenly realized that I had been there for more than an hour and had not even been to the liquor store at the end of the mall for Mom's cigarettes.

I must be in deep trouble now, I thought.

I was so disappointed with myself. I had failed again. I was terrified of what I knew she would do to me.

How could I have been so selfish? How could I have kept Mom from her cigarettes for so long? I felt as if I had deliberately disappointed her.

This was simply unforgivable and would yield a severe lesson for me to remember; I was almost accepting the inevitable before I even got home.

As I ran out of the shop, I suddenly stopped, turned around, and made it a point to walk, not run, back to the table to say thank you and pay my dollar. I had no idea what I was supposed to pay; I always paid one dollar. I ran back out and turned to the right of the doorway where I had laid my bike down and found it gone.

It can't be gone. I felt the blood drain from my face. *I must have misplaced it.*

I was terrified. Not only had I disappointed Mom, but now I'd lost my bike as well. I knew she would be livid.

I walked around the complex, wondering if I had placed it somewhere else. Perhaps I had left it near the bakery where another friend always had the best pastries for me, also at only a dollar. Perhaps it was near the drugstore or the sandwich shop. All my searching was in vain. The bike was nowhere to be found.

I contemplated what I could tell her—anything from being mugged to lending the bike to a friend. That one would never work. I had few friends other than Josh. Even she knew that. She constantly reminded me of my unworthiness to have friends due to my "gross" and "horrible" appearance and my inability to speak.

In a panic, I told the woman in the doughnut shop what had happened. She acted out of kindness, not knowing the cost of what she was about to do, and called the local police to have them file a report for me. As she came back and told me what she had done, I was paralyzed with fear and instant flashes of Mom's face screaming at me: "Never, ever talk to the police unless I'm with you. If you do I'll beat the life right out of you."

Her face scared me more than her words; I knew she meant every word of it. Those vivid instructions never to talk to the police were all I could hear. Over and over those words repeated in my head. Completely avoiding the police was one of Mom's cardinal rules. I really believed that she would kill me if I ever talked to them. Rehearsed over and over, I had to repeat back to Mom: "Never talk to the police!" Just to make sure I understood.

So many nights I was kept up long after the others went to bed and made to repeat: "Never talk to the police. Never talk to the police."

Usually one of Mom's late-night sessions of teaching me all that I'd done wrong that day would close with me being forced to repeat that phrase out loud, but not loud enough to wake anyone else.

"Never talk to the police! Never talk to the police!"

By the time I was ten years old I was petrified of even seeing a police officer.

———————

I begged the woman in the doughnut shop to call back and ask the police to forget about it.

"You don't know what you have done. Please call them back, please, please, please." I begged her with more sincerity than I had ever begged Mom to stop.

I cried as I contemplated my fate. It was too late! There must have been a car in the area because the officer walked in less than a minute after the call was placed and stared at me as he passed. He looked back as if in wonder at the sight of such a dirty boy. I was sure he saw something in me that would give away the secret that Mom and I had been able to keep for years now—our private and all-too-personal life. We both knew it all too well.

At that moment I felt ashamed for Mom—not for me, but for her. This surprised me. It was the first time I had actually felt something for Mom other than pure rage and hate. Although I had had ill feelings all along, I found I felt a sort of sorrow and pity for her as the policeman stared at me.

After a short conversation with my friend in the doughnut shop, the officer walked over to the table where I had been for a few moments and sat down. He was very professional in speech and tone. As he took out a small black notebook and asked what happened, I began my stuttered replies. I was very sure to add "sir" at the end of everything I said, hoping to impress him and not to cause any further suspicion. Talking to him made me so nervous that all I could see was Mom's face screaming at me, *Never talk to the police.* I was sweating in fear, stuttering like never before. He showed me his notebook and what he was writing. I was obviously nervous about what he was writing.

Then came the questions I feared most.

"What's your name, son?"

"My name?"

I was completely shocked. I'd fully expected that he already knew my name, as I was one of the most horrible children in the Bay Area. I did so many things wrong all the time. I failed to complete my chores in time or properly. Mom told me I had an extremely violent temper inside me and that I was unstable. Surely the police knew about me.

"Okay, where do you live?" I could tell he was annoyed with my lack of response.

"Wwww-hhhh-aaaaa-tttt," I blurted out. "I aaaa-mmm-mmm nottttt allowedddd to give thattttt tttoooo yyyy-ooo-uuu, the p-oo-lllll-ice," I stuttered.

I had blown it now. I knew I wasn't supposed to say that. *She is going kill me,* I thought. *I mean actually kill me.* I saw flashes from a few years before, when I saw David weep with terror as she separated his flesh with her fingers in the bathroom. I had thought about that moment so many thousands of times since then, whenever she reminded me: "I can kill you anytime I want to!"

I knew she wasn't kidding. I had seen her try.

I froze when I realized that the last part of my thought had come out of my mouth. The policeman had heard me say that my mother would kill me. He sat back in wonder and took a moment to regain his composure, knowing there was more here than the surface of a little boy in dirty clothes. My heart was pounding right out of my chest. My hands were dripping wet from fear, and I felt the blood rush back to my face.

"What did you say—little man?" the officer demanded.

I looked around for the fastest way to run out. I didn't know what to do—there was no crowd to hide in. As I looked over my shoulder toward the door, I saw my chance. I jumped out of the red leather booth and ran to the door. I could feel the eyes of everyone in the place on me as I ran. I imagined police officers all over asking these people for my description. They would use it to find me and arrest me for running away from them. As I approached the door, a man was just coming in, and he stopped me dead in my tracks. He must have seen the officer behind me and grabbed my arm to hold me until the officer got there. The stranger truly thought he was helping the police out, having no idea what was about to happen. I knew I was dead. I simply slumped inside myself and gave up. Mom would show no mercy. Being caught by the police for running away from them and possibly letting our secret out was an unimaginable crime.

The policeman asked me to sit in the back of his car as he talked to the woman in the doughnut shop. It must have been fifteen minutes before he returned. I waited and imagined my friend breaking down in tears and confessing that she had had no idea I was so bad. She would be distraught at the fact that she'd tried to help someone as loathsome as me. Mom was right. I was worthless.

I thought about the questions the kids at school would ask. All those questions about why I looked as dirty as I did and why I looked like I hadn't slept in days. As I thought about them, I realized just how pitiful my life was.

As people walked by the police car to go about their business, they all looked into the back window. I felt as if I was in a circus, and people were walking by to have a look at the criminal child who'd finally gotten caught. I was so ashamed and so lonely at that moment, I wanted to die.

Without saying a word, the officer came back. He started the car and drove off. I was sure I was going to jail. Perhaps I would see IT and we could talk about old times, I thought. I pictured us in black-and-white-striped clothes with ball and chain, walking with a limp. Although it was a scary thought, I was comfortable with it. I wasn't afraid of it. I was, however, afraid of David and what he might do to get revenge.

Then it hit me. I was going to jail, away from her. Thoughts of the officer being mean and cruel were dissolved by gratitude and joy—even love.

Lost in a daydream about the new home I imagined I was going to, I was quickly brought back to earth as I realized we were turning down Crestline Avenue.

I went crazy, screaming at the officer and begging him not go to my house. I pulled as hard as I could at the door handles of the car, but nothing happened; they were welded shut. He stopped the car near the top of the street and told me in a soft, calm voice that he was here to help, and he would ensure that I wouldn't be hurt. I just couldn't believe him. He had no idea what he was saying, no idea of the pain and the tears that lived in that house, no idea what he was about to create for me. He had no idea what the concrete walls in the basement had already seen, let alone what they were about to see. This time I was beyond fear, I was beyond tears. She would kill me.

As the car stopped in front of our driveway, the officer let me out. I stood behind him as he walked into the open garage, using his body as a shield in the hope that perhaps he would protect me, but I knew he couldn't. No one was in the garage. He told me to follow him as we walked around the front yard and up the pink concrete steps to the front door of Hell itself. We went up one step after another of that long, cold, hard staircase that led to the green door, and her.

As the door opened she was there. The sight of an officer and me together shocked her. She instantly became Mrs. Cleaver. Was I all right, hurt, or scared? I knew that whenever she played the worried mother, she was building up more and more anger inside that she would eventually release, and I would end up with the worst beating of my life. I was cold with panic.

"What on earth happened to my poor boy?" she cried out.

Shortly after Mrs. Cleaver emerged from Mom's assortment of personalities, I was asked to sit in the kitchen as the officer and Mom talked. It seemed like forever before I heard the sound of the door closing and she came into the kitchen. I had resolved to myself that this moment was my last. I wasn't sure how she would do it, but I was convinced that she would send me either to the hospital or, this time, to the morgue. The few moments I had to contemplate this gave me a sense of comfort—until I saw her face.

It was as if she was on fire. Picking up a plate from the counter to use as a shield, I jumped up to run away from her. I tripped on the floor near the refrigerator and slammed my head on the floor. I could feel the tears welling up in my eyes, but I was determined not to cry. I couldn't let her see me cry. If I'd ever had the ability to hold it in, now was the time.

As she screamed at the top of her voice she carefully walked over to the refrigerator. Looking up at her I could see the fire in her bloodshot eyes. As if in slow motion, she started to kick and kick, over and over, kicking my chest, my stomach, and my neck. Even though my eyes held back the tears my body was crying out in pain.

"If you ever tell anyone about me, I will give you the beating of your life. Just who the hell do you think you are? What have I told you, over and over again? You just can't listen to me, can you?

"Can you?"

I knew that drunken evil tone too well.

Kick after kick, the chest and the arms, the face and the neck, she just wouldn't stop.

"Answer me, you miserable worthless piece of shit! *No*—don't you pass out on me. I'm talking to you—don't you pass out!" she screamed at the top of her lungs.

That is the last I recall. I woke to absolute silence some time later. Not a soul was in the kitchen or anywhere else that I could hear. I immediately noticed the smell of my own vomit. I could barely move. My chest felt as if it was crushed. My side was throbbing in pain with every breath. When I lifted my head off the floor, a rush of stars filled my eyes. Dizzy and confused, I simply lay there, wishing someone would come in and help me off the floor. But as always, no one came. No one was there. I was exhausted and alone. Inside I was truly alone. I felt as if I was the only person on the planet.

Within a few minutes, I could hear the basement door open. As she walked in the kitchen, without so much as looking at me she said, "You'd better clean that mess off my floor and be damned quick. Change your shirt, too, you stink!"

I was unable to see clearly from the sweat and vomit on my face and burning in my eyes. With nothing else to use I wiped my face with my arm again and again.

"Go wash up. You make me sick!" she called out from the other room as she walked away.

Finding my way to my feet, I stumbled into the cabinet door just before the kitchen hallway. Holding on to the wall, I felt my way along and found the bathroom. As I reached for the faucet, my arms shook. Resting my arms on the edge of the sink, I heard her calling me.

"Are you done in there? I'm not done with you out here."

The sound of her voice sent me into a crying fit. The tears were from the emotions and the fear. Not from the physical pain but from what was hurting on the inside. My heart was broken. I just didn't care anymore.

Unexpectedly, she came into the bathroom and asked, smugly, if I was going to answer her. As she pulled my head back by my scalp, she looked into my eyes and paused. Then she let go. My head snapped forward and the pain shot down my back. Frozen, with my eyes closed, I expected some sort of slap or kick, but nothing happened. Opening my eyes, I realized she had left. I reached again for the faucet, but my arms just couldn't hold themselves up enough to reach that far. Looking down under the sink, I found my massive laundry pile and pulled out a dirty pair of my briefs. As I wiped my face and neck, the smell was horrific. I folded the underwear over, wiped the front of the shirt I had on, and gave up. I didn't care what I looked like or smelled like. I just wanted to sleep.

I'm so tired and cold. I just want to rest, I thought.

I was so cold and so desperate to breathe fresh air.

Tossing the briefs back into the pile under the sink, I walked out of the bathroom and into my room, fortunately only a few feet away. Looking at the ladder leading to the top bunk, I decided that I didn't have the energy to climb that high. As I turned around I saw the old opening in the collection of junk I had in the middle of the room and crawled inside. All I wanted to do was sleep. But within four minutes, I was summoned to the kitchen again.

Surprisingly, as she finished her glass of vodka, she told me to lie on the couch in the front room until she could get to me. Just before I fell asleep she came in to inform me that I would not be joining "her family" for dinner, and that there would be no school, either. As far as any new school clothes were concerned, I was getting nothing.

Ignoring her futile attempts to get one more dig into me, I simply fell asleep. After the boys had dinner, one of my brothers asked why I was on the couch. With a stern and sharp voice, he was told not to speak to me.

"Just ignore him!" she called out to the other boys.

As I tried to talk to Scott, every breath I took caused more and more pain. I couldn't talk or breathe. Looking around, I couldn't find anybody. No one was there. Once again, I was left to myself, wondering *Where are they, why won't someone help me?*

I must have been lying there for a long time; it was now well past dark and everyone else was in bed. I looked deep into my soul for something to hang on to. I found nothing, except a pool of tears that would never make it to my eyes. Only now the pool was full. I couldn't take it anymore. The thought of no new clothes for school, no one around to help me, then or ever, was too much. I thought of her yelling at me about the clothes I was never going to get, and I decided I wasn't going back to school in the same old things from last year. The pants were three inches higher than the tops of my shoes. The kids called them "floods." The shirt was so dirty and old that it actually smelled, even after I washed it as best I could. I couldn't even see the bottom of the washing machine unless I crawled on top of it; I didn't know how much soap to use, or if I was doing it right.

I mustered up as much strength as I could, being careful not to move too fast, as the pain in my side was so bad. I walked past the front door on my way back to my room and stopped.

The door, I thought.

The door!

I'm alone, no one is here, and I can slip out and leave this miserable place, I thought with the slightest ray of hope.

Since I had already had the police take me home, I was sure I knew how to outsmart them to avoid capture.

I looked in the closet near the front door for a coat, but I found nothing. Daly City got very damp and cold at night.

I'll just go without.

As I opened the door, I thought of my oldest brother, Ross. How would he feel if I left? It didn't matter; I had to leave this place. I was thinking that he was the only one I would miss, and I felt sad inside. Tears began to soak my face.

I start to go down the cold steps. I make my way around to the front yard and down the street. Finding myself getting short of breath, I have to stop. At the end of the street and facing Westmore Hill I realize I can't go any farther without resting. I fall to the steps of the last house on the street. I know some of the kids there and have seen the family before, but I don't know them well enough to call for help. At the same time, I understand that they can't help. No one can. Not even God.

As I make it to my feet, the pain becomes worse. I go across the wide street, to the bottom of the huge hill, and slowly make my way to the top. I know I have to make it to the top. Halfway up I try crawling the rest of the way, as my legs and arms are just too tired and my side hurts too much. The sweat from my face is becoming worse. It feels as if my left eye is sweating by itself; as if water is running down my face from my eye and forehead.

Finally I'm there, at the incinerator of Westmore High School, which I think must be warm. I crawl near the base of the large black tower. I feel the heat and I begin to relax. As I fall asleep, I try to forget about the pain and the cold.

Just end this and let me rest.

"Do you hear me? Are you listening to me?" I demand of God.

I pray for him to take my life and take me away from that place. Take me away from home.

I'm sorry if I never believed in you.
I'm asking you here and now.
Take me home.

"Forgive me, Father, for I have sinned . . ."

It is the only prayer I know. Over and over in my head, I say: "Forgive me, Father."

But like my father on earth, my father in heaven isn't interested in me, either.

As I wake to unfamiliar sounds, I see a large man in a blue uniform asking me what the hell I'm doing there. I try to jump to my feet but I only fall back down again from the pain in my side. My entire body is sore and frozen. It must be 6:00 A.M. or so, long before school is supposed to start. I get back up before he can grab me. I try to run to the top of the hill, falling and getting back up, running while trying to put all the weight on my left side. It is considerably less painful now. Going down the steep hill toward home, I fall to the grass and roll down the rest of the hill on my side, crying out in pain. The pain is now making me sick; I vomit at the bottom of the hill, all over my pants and shoes. The smell is so bad that I get sick from getting sick. I know I'm in trouble this time.

When she sees me and realizes that I left last night she is going to go crazy.

I don't care, I'm tired, I'm cold, and my head is pounding and my heart is shattered.

"I just want to die," I softly say.

I make my way back to the house. I don't know where else to go. I walk past my neighbors' windows wondering if they can see this pathetic little boy hobbling up the street, soaked in puke and smelling like it. I realize I don't care what she is going to do to me. I stop at the bottom of the stairs and hear one of my brothers cry out.

"There he is!"

I make it up the steps and to the door when she suddenly opens the door and grabs my arm, pulling me inside and onto the floor. Screaming at the top of her lungs: "Where in the hell were you? Who saw you? What did they say?

"Tell me—*Tell me!*"

I don't care anymore. I just want to sleep. To my amazement she stands there looking down at me on the floor. Silence cuts through the room. The expression on her face changes, from evil to almost human. As she carefully picks me up and places me on the couch I feel the warmth of her body and I'm at ease for a moment. I can smell the faded scent of perfume and feel the ever-so-soft skin of her face. As she lays me down I am comforted that she has been concerned about me. She does not say it—I can feel it. The look on her face and the fear in her eyes for me is something I can only recall in distant memories. I'm happy to be with her for that moment—just that moment.

The boys had all gathered around and were asking her all kinds of questions, at which her temper flared. At the first sign of her temper everyone left the room. I thought I was going to get it now. I couldn't have moved if I'd wanted to. I could barely breathe from that point on.

This is it, here it comes.

Just take it, Richard—just take it.
I have no fear of you now!
I have nothing left to give you, or anyone else.
I have nothing that can be taken from me, either.
"I'm done!" I whisper.

To my complete amazement she simply looked at me, smiled, and walked away. Soon my brothers came back into the living room and stared at me. Scott was asking dumb questions, trying to make fun of me, as I was helpless to defend myself. This perfect opportunity to home in for the kill was just too much for him to pass up. I recalled how it must have felt for David. I was hurt by his need to pursue my pain. I also knew exactly how he felt. I'd felt the same when I'd looked at David in his anguish.

Then he realized that it hurt when I tried to speak. He started to say things that would make me laugh. Not to take my mind off the situation, but to cause pain. I tried not to laugh; the pain was too much. At one point I rolled over, reacting to the sharp stabbing pain in my chest, and fell to the floor from the sofa. I couldn't move. I couldn't breathe; I thought I was going to be sick again. I was still wearing the shirt covered in puke and dirt. I got sick again. This time it was on her carpet and on the side of my face. I could feel the mess in my ears and in my hair. The entire side of my face was covered and the smell was worse than before. Heaving dry spells again and again, each twist of my body caused more pain and convulsions.

As she walked down the hallway, she called my name at the top of her voice and told me to get back on the couch. I couldn't respond. I could hear her, but I just couldn't respond. I couldn't really see clearly as my eyes were filled with tears and sweat. I turned my head to the side, because I knew I was about to be sick again. I didn't want the mess in my eyes. They hurt too badly now. After I vomited again she came over, knelt down close to my face, looked me in the eyes, and said: "Oh my God! I'm calling an ambulance."

She almost appeared to be concerned for me. For a moment I assumed she was afraid I would die.

7

AN AMBULANCE RIDE

I had been to the hospital several times before, and even watched as my older brother had another cast placed on his arm or his leg. The hospital didn't frighten me; I was used to being there. But this time was different. I was alone and completely comfortable being away from Mom. The experience helped me start to form a separation from Mom, a separation that would take many years to come to fruition.

S LOW DOWN, I thought.

Then it hit me: I wasn't crying; why would I have tears? I had been completely focused on showing her I wasn't going to cry. No matter how bad it got, I wasn't going to show her it hurt. Now I could feel the tears coming from my left eye, but as I reached my hand up to wipe it, the pain was unbearable and I cried out. When I pulled my hand down to look, I realized that it was not tears coming out of my eye; it was blood.

She knelt down and asked me not to tell "them" what had happened. Wiping my face and the top of my shirt with a wet cloth, she tried to remove the vomit that had been there for hours.

"Who? Tell who?" I hesitantly asked.

"The paramedics, they're on the way to help you. If they think I did this they will take you from me," she calmly replied.

She was so sincere and so concerned about it that I felt a duty to protect the ongoing secret and keep her from being embarrassed about it. The expression on her face was touching. The dependency and the fear in her voice burned into my mind. It was as if my trustworthiness was now being tested. I had to help her. At that moment I felt bad for her— not for me, but for her. I felt embarrassed and ashamed for her. It was hard for me to understand where these feelings were coming from. It was almost impossible to believe that I was concerned for her and not me.

I took pity on her. Somehow this gave me power. I was in control now and she knew it. I was the one who could strike the fear of God into her. I was confused.

As I contemplated my response to her plea for silence, the paramedics arrived. One knelt by my side and started talking to me. The other immediately started talking on the radio to someone else. The rush of questions fired at me confused me even further and I stuttered any words I could get out between the pains. After a moment I realized I was making little sense to them. The paramedic put his hand over my mouth and told me to calm down, breathe, and relax. As I looked around for Mom, she was nowhere in sight.

Before long I was on the gurney, being rolled to the front door. She attempted to stop one of the paramedics in the front of the gurney and ask a question. Without losing a step they simply ignored her as if she wasn't even there.

I found satisfaction in that. Now she knew how humiliated it made me feel to be completely ignored on a daily basis, as if I didn't even exist. As we turned, I realized that I was being carried down the front steps on the long gurney, and I became frightened. I tried to call out to the two men and tell them to stop because I was afraid they would drop me, but the words never came. For the first time I found myself unable to say anything at all. The desire and the will were there, but not the action. I was horrified. Harder and harder I tried. It became more difficult to breathe. I was trying to breathe faster and faster in order to cry out: *Don't drop me, please!*

The paramedics stopped at the bottom of the steps and reached into one of the bags at my feet. A plastic mouthpiece was placed on my face. I was sure it was to keep me quiet as we passed the people and neighbors out on their lawns and the sidewalks, looking on uncertainly. I could only imagine them wondering what I had done now. They must have imagined something terrible. The embarrassment of being gagged as I was carried out into the ambulance overwhelmed me.

Inside the ambulance a kind of comfort came over me, calm and quiet.

"You're hyperventilating. You need to slow down! Breathe into the mask—slowly," the man in the ambulance sternly told me.

I looked out the side window as we drove off and was able to see Mom yelling at two of my brothers.

She can't even wait until I'm dead before she starts on a new one, I thought.

I became angry, very angry. The paramedic saw my state and began to hold me down on the mattress. I thought he was trying to comfort me. I had no idea what he said to me.

She is already starting in on a new victim. It was all I could think of.

It was just like when IT left. Only now, she couldn't even wait the three whole days of reprieve that I'd been given. She showed no concern for me. I was gone. I was out of her life.

To her, I'm already dead!

The paramedic's hold on my arm became stronger until I finally noticed the force and the pressure he was applying. My thoughts changed, and I now was aware of only him. He had my full attention.

"You must do as I say or I can't help you," he said.

Can't help me! You have no idea what you have done, taking me out of that house. I tried to say the words but they wouldn't come.

I couldn't speak.

I'm as good as dead to her now!

"Now I can never show her I really am a good boy!" I finally stuttered.

His grip on my arm became more painful as he grabbed my other arm and yelled to the driver up front. I don't re-member what he said; at that moment I couldn't understand him. As I looked him in the eyes I realized I was sitting up and attempting to hit him in the face and shoulders. I was shocked. I had been acting out my anger and wasn't even aware of it.

Suddenly the back door opened and the driver came in. The ambulance was stopped somewhere on the way to wherever we were going. The other paramedic held me as the first paramedic gave me a shot in the arm. I reacted violently, but this time I knew what I was doing. I had no reason to act that way. I knew they were there to help. I was so confused at what was happening around me I finally broke down and cried.

I was mad at Mom and I was frightened at being alone. The two men who were trying to help me just confused me and made me feel helpless. I was becoming overwhelmed with the flood of thoughts that now filled my head. The anger and shame of being in this position only added to my state. Of all the emotions, what I felt the most was embarrassment.

A few moments after the shot in the arm, I relaxed. The pain between breaths was weakening. I could focus and understand the paramedic sitting next to me as he kept talking to me. He had the softest and lowest voice I had ever heard from a man before. It was as if we had been friends for years and he was telling me secrets no one else should hear. I don't recall what he said, but it was all so comforting. I could tell he was becoming concerned about me and seemed to be as anxious as I was.

I watched him as he put his hand on my shoulder, rubbing my shoulder and looking at the driver. Over and over he kept changing from looking at the driver to looking at me. There was a worry in his eyes. I knew by his expression that something was wrong.

I realized that he was genuinely concerned for me and wanted to help.

I began to picture Mom back home: God only knew what she was doing to whom. My thoughts leapt from remembering hitting the paramedic, back to Mom at home, and back to the paramedic, over and over. I thought for a moment that perhaps she was right. I was a "no good kid" and "not worth the time of day," as she always had told me. Maybe she had been right all along. No little boy would react the way I had done to the paramedic who was trying to help me when I needed it most.

I have no right to be a part of Mom's family, I thought as I fell asleep. I was disappointed in myself.

I had no idea where I was or what was happening around me when I jolted awake. All kinds of people were now surrounding me. They were everywhere. After a moment, I recognized my surroundings. I was in the hospital emergency room. I felt so tired. I needed to sleep, but I was too upset. Fear and exhaustion were the only feelings I could muster. Again, everybody was asking me a hundred questions all at once.

I tried to speak but couldn't. I couldn't even stutter. Feeling brokenhearted, cold, dirty, and embarrassed, I just lay there quietly, ignoring everyone and feeling ashamed. Then I became aware of what was happening around me. I began to feel angry.

Freezing-cold water was poured on my face and dripped behind my ears as it ran down the back of my shirt. The bed they had just moved me onto became soaked as another bottle was opened and handed to the man nearest my head. One bottle of water after another was poured on me until I was completely soaked. My shirt was removed with a pair of scissors. Without knowing why, I could feel anger building and building inside me. Real anger—something I had not felt before. All I wanted was to get back home and out of where I was. I had to see if Mom was in trouble as a result of my breaking my silence. I had to see if she needed me to lie for her again and cover up for her. I didn't want her to be left alone. I felt bad for her.

I tried to ignore the questions being fired at me. I ignored their talking to one another. I was angry and scared at the same time.

Then it hit me all at once, like a train running out of control:

Back home? I never want to go back!

The thoughts in my head confused me. All the emotions that I had buried so deep and for so long were now filling my heart.

My thoughts went back and forth from anger to the fear of going home. Back and forth, faster and faster everything raced in my head.

My mind was spinning out of control. The emotions were now near the surface, and I knew that if I didn't control myself, I would let them out. I could never allow that to happen. No one must ever see any emotion from me, ever.

I knew that I was close to losing all control. The fear, the pain, the anger, the love, the pity, and the remorse were all running from my heart to my head too fast.

I tried to focus and think of the cold, hard walls in the basement and the emotions and the tears only they knew. They had seen all the unspeakable events and they were hiding them better than I ever could have.

Try to be like the walls, cold and silent.

Cold and silent.

Cold and silent. Over and over I quietly repeated this to myself.

I was so confused and ashamed that I tried to get up and away from everyone around me. I didn't realize that my arms and legs had fallen asleep. As I tried harder and harder to move, the doctors noticed my struggles.

Off to my right was an older woman who talked to me in a soft, low voice. I couldn't remember what she said, only the soft and controlled tone of her voice. I reacted to the sound as if it was the calm before the storm I was so accustomed to. It was the voice that would lead to the pain inflicted by Mom. The voice that was forever burned in my mind, like a scar that will never go away.

"No!

"No!

"No!" I finally cried out.

The doctor at the foot of the bed stopped talking to the people around him just as I finished the last "no." He quickly walked over to my side and asked the woman to my right for something. I had no idea what she was told and watched in fear as she stepped away from me, took something from the tall metal cart at the foot of the bed, and then returned. She handed the doctor whatever she had obtained from the cart. I realized that he was going to do something to me as he came closer and closer and I panicked.

I managed to sit up quickly and raise my arms to cover my head and face—a reaction I had mastered. The pain actually forced me to stop. From the bottom of my legs I could feel the pain run up my back and across my chest. Every piece of skin on my body tingled as if it was being poked. It felt like an elephant was sitting on my chest—I had to give up. The noise from everyone talking around me, at me, and to me wore me out. I couldn't listen anymore. I couldn't think anymore.

I was beaten.

I was done.

There was nothing I could do and I had no further will to fight.

Stars began to cover my vision, the blood rushed to my head, and I fell unconscious. Before I lost awareness I could see the woman and the doctor on either side of me holding me down. There was someone new at the foot of the bed holding my legs, and another new face was now holding my head. This doctor gave me a shot of something in my neck.

Whatever it was, whatever he gave me, it worked—I was done. Within a moment I felt nothing. I could barely see and had no concern for the commotion going on around me. The sounds became softer and softer as the light faded to darkness.

All I could see was stars. I had no idea what happened after I passed out.

To this day I have never been told.

———

I woke several hours later bathed and in a clean, warm bed, without any signs of blood, dirt, or tears. I was wearing a large bandage on my eye, which covered half my face, some kind of tight vest around my chest, and white cotton bandages on my hands and knees. I looked down at my legs and saw the scrapes on my feet and the blisters from shoes that had grown too small six months before. Blisters that no boy should have. I could see through the thin hospital clothes I had draped over me and I realized I was completely undressed—I didn't even have my underwear on. I thought for a moment that I would be embarrassed by it but quickly changed my mind when I realized the comfort of my current surroundings—peace and quiet, soft lights, and Mom nowhere in sight.

For the first time in my life, a sigh came out of nowhere— not just any sigh, but the sigh of relief. I felt better as I fell back to sleep.

It has been a long time, I thought.

This time I'll sleep with my eyes closed, I decided.

———

Morning started a little earlier than I'd hoped. The hospital was still and quiet. As I woke, a beautiful young woman spoke softly to me and rubbed my hair. Careful of my face, she didn't touch the bandages placed there.

"You know you can't sleep forever," she said with a smile.

I smiled back at her.

I felt like she should be my mom. My sense of security seemed false as she told me that I was going to be released eventually and would have to go back home. I immediately noticed that as she talked to me, she was very careful to ask me about my feelings and my thoughts.

I had been training myself to watch Mom's emotions and listen to her tone of voice. I knew the pretty woman sitting at my bedside wanted something from me. I found it odd that a stranger would be concerned about me. After all, I was "nothing."

She was being genuine and I confided in her that I was comfortable and would try to speak slower and not stutter as I spoke. She smiled back at me.

"It's okay—I understand," she said calmly.

She made me feel good when she complimented me on my freckles and red hair.

"You must make the girls silly with your good looks." She laughed.

I could feel the redness in my face, not from pain but from a sense of embarrassment.

I've found a friend.

She told me she would be right back as she walked out of the room. Stopping suddenly, looking back, she reassured me that she would really be back.

"Promise!" she exclaimed.

I had never thought about a girl liking me before, let alone thinking of me as "cute." I was embarrassed beyond belief. As she had promised, she returned with a large tray of food. It smelled good and I could see that it was hot. She opened the top and I saw eggs, toast and jelly, a few pieces of bacon, and some juice. Though she told me to eat only what I thought I could and not to worry if I couldn't finish, I ate the whole thing. I polished off every piece as she watched, amazed. It was then that I noticed that she wasn't wearing what I would have expected a nurse to wear at a hospital. She was in slacks and a shirt. I wasn't sure if she was a nurse or not. It didn't matter to me. I was comfortable for a change.

"If you keep eating like that you'll be out of here in no time," she reminded me.

I immediately apologized for what I had done, and said I wasn't thinking and that I had forgotten my manners. I so wanted to impress her, as she was now my friend.

"It's okay. It's all right," she reassured me.

As I stared out the window at the sunshine, I tried desperately to enjoy the moment. It became harder and harder to deliberately and consciously keep Mom and the others back home out of my mind.

This is my moment!

Why can't I have my own peace? I thought.

Before long, I fell asleep to the feeling of the sunshine as it warmed me all over. It's a feeling that to this day can soothe and comfort me.

"Well, do you think you can just lie around all day here, young man?"

As the words rang in my head, I sat up as fast as possible and thought of what it was I was supposed to be doing and what excuse I was going to instantly blurt out. I was unsure where I was and why I was sleeping. I was confused.

"I'm sorry. I fell asleep. I'm sorry," I sheepishly pronounced.

Once her face came into focus, I realized it was my friend, the woman who had helped me and had made me feel so comfortable.

I could see confusion come over her face as she watched my immediate reaction and my ability to go from a dead sleep to fully awake and stuttering in a flash. She quickly and deliberately changed her facial expression.

"It's okay," she apologized.

She startled me.

"I didn't mean to upset you."

As I felt myself getting embarrassed and turning red again, she came over to hold my arm and hand. Running her fingers through my hair, she started talking softly about anything, anything at all.

"You know, I was told that you stutter all the time and would be hard to understand.

"Now, where do you think they got such a silly idea as that, I wonder?"

As I listened to her question, I realized that I wasn't embarrassed about stuttering around her. I was speaking clearly and without hesitation. Amazed at myself, I couldn't believe that she was right and I hadn't even noticed.

"I don't know!" I shyly replied.

I was trying to play along with the idea of stuttering being silly and how "immature" it would be. As the conversation went on, she sat down on the side of the bed and said: "Richard—I have to tell you something. Your mother is here to pick you up."

Every feeling of love, comfort, warmth, and every soft-spoken word I had just absorbed fell out of me. It was as if I had dropped the dishes, shattering them into a million pieces of trash that could never be put back together.

"Is there something you want to tell me? Is there something that I should know about what happened? I can help you, you know.

"I have a feeling that things are not the way they are supposed to be at home and I would be upset if you did not tell me. Please tell me," she begged.

As her questions sat in the forefront of my mind, I flashed back to Mom's awful breath as she screamed in my face: "You'd better not tell anyone, especially the police!"

Looking for a response, she pulled my face up from my chest and asked again. I groped for an answer but I couldn't find one. I wanted to scream: *You bet your ass there is!*

But I could only listen to myself as I quietly said: "No. Everything's fine."

"Richard? You're not telling me the truth, are you?" she demanded.

"You don't understand! You just don't understand!" I begged back at her.

As she stood up and gathered my things on the tray for me, she looked back down at me and quietly said: "Very well."

I had the worst feeling of letting my new friend down. Once again I had failed. I tried to understand and decided that perhaps if I just let her know a little bit about Mom, then maybe Mom wouldn't get in a lot of trouble. Maybe Mom would just get in a little trouble and would change if she felt bad about what she was doing to me. Mustering up as much courage as I could possibly find, I stammered: "You kk-nnn-o-wwww, I-I-I- thi-nnnnn-k th-aaaa-t I wannnn-t to sa-yyyy sommmmm-thi-ng."

I realized that I turned back into the little boy who couldn't speak—the Freak, as Mom would say, "the poor excuse for a child."

I shoved my chin deep into my chest and froze. She turned to me, knelt, lifted my head, and said: "Yes? What is it?"

All I could do, more embarrassed than ever, was acknowledge that I was just a little worthless boy. All I could do was shake my head and softly say: "No. Never mind."

As I walked out of the room, I held my head low and felt worse inside than on the outside. We turned the corner and there she was.

I was sick. My stomach turned and I felt as if I was going to vomit.

Mom was sitting in the waiting area like a proud father after the news of an arrival in the delivery room. Her eyes lit up as they met my own. I saw her face and I returned to hanging my head deep in my chest as I walked with her to the car. Not a word was spoken between us.

I was beaten.

She won.

The ride back to the house was more than an hour long. Occasionally, Mom would look through the mirror at me in the backseat. The cold and twisted glance she gave me told me that she had won once again. She had made it out of another encounter with the authorities unscathed. Not long into the quiet drive home, I was sure that I heard her talking to herself: "What an idiot. He thought he was getting away. Well—I'll fix that!"

We each knew that the secret was still safe. I had fulfilled my family obligation and was worthy of her trust. Just knowing that I was going back with her was enough to make me cry. Even if I was only crying on the inside, I resolved to myself that I would never let her see me cry again—ever.

8

THE GUN

I was already emotionally and mentally drained. Yet my mind was spinning faster than I could keep up with. The one thought that kept me awake was how to stop Mom from harming me. I had to find a way to end the abuse. I was pretty sure I couldn't find the guts to stand up to her, so there had to be another way.

I knew it was there and I knew I could easily find it. What I didn't know was that I couldn't go through with it. I was afraid to actually kill her. I recall only a few times—when I was walking in the grove near school, or every now and again after a severe beating—hearing that voice inside me. I wasn't sure if it was my conscience or something divine. Whatever it was, it was familiar to me. Not familiar like I experienced it all the time, but familiar like when I listened to the radio and thought I've heard that song before, *yet it was brand-new.*

WHAT WOULD CHANGE? Watching her driving and talking to herself, all I could think of was what I might do to change my life.

What can I do?

What if I stopped her—but how?

As I looked out the window and tried to think, I started to doze off. The more I tried to keep my thoughts clear, the more exhaustion overcame me.

I have to stop her. I have to end this nightmare once and for all.

Within a moment that familiar feeling came over me once again, as if I wasn't alone; as if there was hope. I had experienced it a few times before and now it was back.

Poison? I wondered. *What about the cleaners she once used to mix to try to kill David? Or I can push her down the stairs.*

The thoughts running through my mind suddenly stopped, overpowered again by that familiar feeling. I can only describe it as an intervention. Someone or something inside me was telling me, even in my situation, to stop. My heart was racing and my mind was spinning faster and faster. The reality of what I was now contemplating sent adrenaline throughout my body.

This is wrong! You know that! I told myself.

"Remember—remember," were the words ringing in my head. I kept hearing these words over and over.

Remember what? What am I supposed to remember?

The rest of the ride I tried to clear my head and think.

Remember what?

Just before we crossed into Daly City, calmness came over me, calmness that I found familiar.

It was that still small voice I had heard on the few occasions I really needed help. That same voice I had heard in the trees walking to school. I had long forgotten about that simple guiding voice. Now it was telling me: "You'll throw your life away. You knew this wasn't going to be easy. I'll be with you."

Was I imagining it, or was it possible—an intervention?

Was it God? Had he finally heard me?

I was humbled and angry at the same time. I was humbled by the idea that finally my prayers for help had been answered. I was angry at the thought that it had taken this long.

Well—it's too late, I decided, and with that, the voice was gone.

I had a sudden realization that there was nobody who would or even could help me now. The nurse had offered to go to bat for me, if I had only had the courage to speak up—but I didn't. I'd had the perfect opportunity to get out, and once again I had failed. I somehow turned from being disappointed in myself to being merely infuriated. How could Mom have had such a hold on me without even being present at the hospital? It was my opportunity to outwardly fight back. Sure, in my mind I had many times conquered her, but the triumph was imaginary. I needed more—far more.

Why not just do it once and for all? I asked myself. *Stop dreaming about it and just do it.* I was arguing with myself, inside my head.

I wanted to find a way out. I wanted freedom. I wanted to just be left alone and have the chance to grow up like a normal kid.

I have to stop her. How do I remove her grip on my soul?

The answer was one I knew was wrong in every sense of the word—"Revenge."

What do I have to lose? I asked myself.

Not long after we arrived home, she drank herself into another stupor and couldn't function enough to walk down the hallway, but made it to her bed. As I lay in my bed, my previous thoughts filled my head.

I was now overwhelmed with the all-too-real need to end the fear and the pain. The thoughts came more and more vividly; every act of violence, every moment of shame was replayed in my head.

The scary part was that I didn't hesitate. I was at peace, relaxed and calm. The whole thing took less than half an hour, from the moment I took my father's black revolver out of his boot, walked over to Mom's bedside, put the gun to the base of her skull—I stopped.

If I do this—what will happen to me?

If I do this—I'll lose everything.

I'll lose myself, my chance to show everyone that I'm truly a good kid.

The words kept coming back to me over and over in my mind: "You'll throw your life away."

Within a moment came that familiar feeling again. It was the calmness I had experienced before.

I knew I wasn't alone. As I stood in Mom's room, someone or something was standing there with me.

In the middle of the act of taking a life, not just any life, but my mother's miserable life—I wasn't alone. The fear inside me grew and became more than I'd ever known. I had the opportunity and the means. Now I finally had the guts.

"Richard—you'll go to Hell if you do this!"

I'm in Hell and she is the one who deserves to be there! I thought back to that still small voice inside me.

I raised the gun to the base of her skull again and slowly pulled the hammer back, locking it in place. The sound of the metal as it locked tight cut through the room. Even the air was motionless. The moments became like hours and the fear became calmness. The anxiety became rest—I was comfortable.

Complete silence filled the room, like the morning fog as it slowly moves in covering the bay. I looked down at my hand, expecting it to be trembling, and found myself calm.

I closed my eyes and squeezed the trigger.

My heart raced as time stood still, anticipating the sound of the shot. I waited and waited. It seemed like minutes when it was only fragments of a second.

The silence hung in the air until all I could hear was the blood rushing through my ears. The adrenaline flowed like water through a fire hose.

As I opened my eyes, I realized that I hadn't put enough pressure on the trigger to drop the hammer. When I looked down and saw that, the still small voice spoke out, but this time it wasn't the soft, calm voice I had heard before inside my head.

The voice was actually in the room. It filled the air like a shout, but was quiet at the same time.

"Stop right now and walk away!" the voice said to me.

The voice was just as real as my own. The fear of pulling the trigger was now overshadowed by the fear that filled my heart, and filled the room.

There was someone else in the room with me. I couldn't see who or what it was. I couldn't find anyone in the room other than Mom and me, but I felt someone's presence. Just like the way I knew when Mom was standing by my bedside though I had the covers pulled tight up over my head. I couldn't see her—I just knew she was there. I knew someone or something was standing right beside me.

I stood motionless.

I thought I heard David downstairs.

I thought I heard the nurse at the hospital ask me if I was all right.

Suddenly I thought both Josh and I were walking to the path of trees by Westmore Hill on our way to school.

What's happening to me? I wondered in fear.

I can't think! I can't breathe. I can't do anything.

I was terrified. I had been frightened before, but never to this point of deep terror from inside my own thoughts.

I quietly and reluctantly listened to that still small voice. I knew I had to.

Why am I forced to stop while she is allowed to carry on, cheating me, cheating my brothers, and cheating you—"God"! I said to myself.

Then I realized that God had nothing to do with this.

I shook my head and tried to clear the cobwebs that filled my thoughts. I searched again for that desire to follow through with what I was about to do. I lifted my thumb off the handle and found the hammer of the gun. As I felt the pressure against my thumb, I knew it would take only a moment to drop the hammer, and it would be over. No more pain, no more tears, no more hurt, no more begging the concrete in the basement for understanding, no more wasted prayers—no more Mom.

I wasn't sure if it was me, or if it was God, but someone took the desire to kill away from me and replaced it with remorse. I simply stood there, motionless and empty.

I had no anger.

I had no fear.

For a moment, I felt nothing. I didn't feel empty. I actually emotionally touched and felt the surface of "nothing." For the first time I truly felt the absence of any emotion—nothing.

I shamelessly walked away from Mom's bedside, put the gun back in my father's work boot, and went to bed.

The sweat from my forehead dripped down my face and burned my eyes. As I awoke in my bed I was startled and confused.

Did I do that? Or was I asleep. What have I done?

I couldn't tell if what woke me was the afterthought of what I had just done or a dream. I didn't remember. I didn't want to.

9

THE LAST BETRAYAL

My life thus far had been void of much, and yet it was full of more than most people could even conceive. As I looked back on the last few years I could only pore over the things I had gone through and think of them as if they were a play that I was watching, connecting with the feelings and the thoughts of the actors as they played their roles. But now, at the age of nine, I looked back and found something more, something else that helped shape me into who I am now.

I had to find that one event, the one event that formed what I was becoming and how I dealt with the years of horror afterward. It was the betrayal of my older brother IT and the years of torment that I caused him. It was now time to come to terms with my life and who I had become.

A T NINE, I was confident that I would never see David's face again. I was sure that between Mom, her hatred for David, and David's own ill feelings for me, it would never happen. I had lost the chance to simply say *I'm sorry.*

Would he understand? Would he even care? These were questions that only he could answer. And now I would never have the chance to ask my brother if he could find enough room in his heart to forgive me.

Not long after David was taken out of the house and placed in foster care, Mom made it clear that if any of us ever saw him around, we were to report it to her immediately. She made it sound as if he were a real threat; he would come after us and harm us. Mom was very insistent that David had serious anger toward the family and especially toward me. She had told me several times, "He'll find a way to get back at you. He's violent and God only knows what he is capable of now."

The thought of seeing him frightened me more than Mom ever did. I knew that if he had the opportunity, he would lash out at me for all the suffering I had caused him. I was terrified of David now.

All I really knew was what Mom had told me, that he had been placed in some kind of prison or "halfway house" somewhere outside Daly City, California. I had no idea where. I didn't even know if he could come back to school.

Will he be waiting for me in the school hallways, lurking and patiently stalking me, looking for payback? I wondered.

As fate would have it, that day finally arrived.

I was walking between classes and heard my name being called from afar. I looked around, but I couldn't make out who was calling or even if he was actually calling me. Then, as I continued to walk, he emerged out of the crowd. It was David.

I was instantly terrified. The thoughts of what Mom had said, and the fear of him being free and looking to get me, gripped me. I assumed he had a knife or, worse, a gun. As he walked up to me I began to shake with fear. All I could think about was his anger toward me; his desire to pay me back for the harm I had caused him.

As soon as he spoke, I knew that he wasn't angry. He seemed almost glad to see me. He had on clean clothes and shoes that looked like they fit. For a moment he looked clean. The look of hunger was gone. He looked—happy.

Confused, I wasn't sure if he was setting me up or if it was genuine happiness. Happiness had not been a normal thing to see in David's face. In fact, it was an expression that I couldn't ever recall being on his face before.

He only had a moment and asked if we could meet tomorrow in the halls and just chat for a while. All I could think of to say was, "Sure."

I was still expecting him to turn around and shoot me.

Just as quickly as I had seen him, he was gone.

Then I realized that he had set me up. He wanted to make sure that I would be at school, and now I'd agreed to see him the next day.

Throughout the day all I could think about was what Mom had said about him and how I should be careful around him if I ever saw him again.

By the time I got home all I could think about was whether I was going to tell Mom and ask for her help. It weighed heavily on my mind. If she was right, then I was in serious danger. If she was wrong, then why would David come to see me? If Mom was wrong and David really was just checking to see if I was all right, then I had nothing to worry about.

After dinner, and with my chores done, I made up my mind.

"I saw David at school today," I told her.

Her anxious reply didn't take long.

"Where?"

Her expression and tone of voice brought me back to years before, when David was kept in the basement like an animal. Her voice was exactly like that, full of hatred and evil.

"What did he say? Where did you see him? Did anyone see you?"

I was frightened and confused by the speed of her questions, as if I was supposed to be able to rattle off the answers immediately. I found myself just as I was years before, stuttering my responses out of fear.

She noticed my expression and suddenly changed her own. A short silence filled the room. Standing and looking at one another, neither of us spoke for a moment.

Mom's excitement over me seeing David convinced me that she was right. David was out to get me.

She had done it. David was out of her life and she had managed to make him the enemy, the one we all should be afraid of—and I was afraid.

Her expression turned from evil to cunning. She knew she had my emotions in the palm of her hand. She made me feel as if she was the only one who could help me.

She walked over to me and I cringed. Expecting to be slapped or kicked, I closed my eyes and the seconds passed as if they were hours. Eventually she knelt down to look at me face-to-face and placed her hands on my shoulders.

Immediately I opened my eyes and was horrified that she was that close to me. I had let her touch me and wasn't prepared to run and shield myself.

Her tone was soft and her face was mellowed. Her breath reeked of alcohol. All I could think of was the smell of her breath.

"You need to listen to me—he's dangerous. There is no telling what he is capable of now," she said with sincerity.

As I listened, I became more afraid of David than of her. It became obvious that she took satisfaction from the fact that I was now frightened of him far more than of her. I was more afraid of seeing him again than anything Mom had done, or would ever do, to me.

Perhaps it was her plan all along.

"What time does he want to see you?" she asked.

"The same time as yesterday, right after the bell," I said.

"I'll take care of that," she said with a familiar tone as she stood up.

I was instructed to go down to the office shortly before the bell and meet Mom there. She said she would be there to protect me when David was "looking for" me at school.

That night as I attempted to sleep, I couldn't determine if Mom was there to protect me from him or if David was actually trying to reach out and protect me from her. All I wanted was both of them out of my mind and out of my life. I was so scared I couldn't sleep.

I tried desperately to understand David's need to see me.
What if Mom's wrong? I wondered.

How could David know that I have fallen into the same trap he was in for all those years?

How could he know what's happened to me? Even when he was in the house, he never showed any concern for me. Why would he show concern for me now? After all, I was the one who had added to his plight—and besides, he had his own fears now.

Or was it possible that even after everything I had done to him, he cared enough to realize that it wasn't really me. It was Mom trying to control me, just like she was doing now with Scott.

Now it makes sense, I realized. *I'm not the horrible Little Nazi. It's* her, *not me.*

She was the one who caused the hurt and the pain. She was the one who didn't care. She was the one who had put me through hell. She was the one who caused David to go away.

Maybe I'm not so bad.

Maybe David isn't, either.

And now I'd set him up. Mom would be there in the morning and he had no way of knowing.

I didn't know what to do.

Should I tell Mom it was all a lie?

Will she believe me?

Could she possibly pass up an opportunity to harass David one last time?

Over and over these questions ran through my mind as I fell asleep.

As morning broke I got myself ready and made what I could for breakfast, unnoticed. *Perhaps she has forgotten about it and I can pretend I never told her.*

As I gathered my books and lunch box, she stopped me in the hallway, grabbed my arm, and pulled me into the kitchen. Then, without any warning, she spun me around to face the refrigerator and said:

"Don't you look at me! You make me sick!"

Confused at what I had done, I could see out of the corner of my eye that she had the kitchen cabinet open and was pulling something from the top shelf. I couldn't tell what it was until she spun me around again.

As she turned me back to facing the living room, I could see what she had in her hand. It was a twelve-ounce bottle of Tabasco sauce.

"I didn't say anything bad!" I cried out.

With tears running down my face, I anticipated the taste of the Tabasco. Tabasco had become one her favorite tools she used to punish me. I couldn't count the number of twelve-ounce bottles she had used on me. The smell and the taste were petrifying. Originally she had started to use the Tabasco whenever she caught me swearing or talking back to her. As soon as she saw its effect on me and how afraid I was of it, she made sure to use it often. Eventually she started using it as punishment for what I was "about to do wrong."

"Never you mind about that!" she barked back at me. "This is to remind you that you had better not say anything at all, you little shit!"

She opened the kitchen drawer, reached for a tablespoon, then suddenly tossed it back into the drawer. She pulled out an oversized serving spoon and filled it with Tabasco.

"Open up, *now!*"

Crying, I reluctantly opened my mouth and closed my eyes. The anticipation of the smell and the taste made me ill. I knew that I had better listen or it was only going to get worse for me. With a sense of determination she shoved the spoon deep in my mouth and pulled it back out across the top of my teeth as she lifted the spoon high to make sure that I got it all.

I tried not to swallow. The taste in my mouth became more than I could handle. I knew I had to swallow it. If I spit it out, I would get twice as much.

As soon as I opened my eyes after swallowing the sauce, they began to swell. The burning of the Tabasco as it went down my throat wasn't half as bad as when it made it to my stomach. I started to feel sick.

"Open up again," she commanded.

I couldn't believe it. She was pouring another spoonful. I tried to speak and give some reason why she should stop, but as soon as I opened my mouth she shoved in the next dose.

When I swallowed the second spoonful, my mouth started watering. The saliva ran out of my mouth and onto my shirt. The tears in my eyes were soaking my face. They were from the taste of the Tabasco, not from the fear.

I could barely see and was trying not to get sick as she said: "One more—honey."

I just couldn't do it. I placed my hands over my face to block the oncoming spoon. Unintentionally, I knocked the spoon out of her hand and the Tabasco sauce spilled on the floor. The fury in her eyes and her heavy breathing let me know I was in even deeper trouble. I could smell the vodka as she breathed heavier and heavier with anger.

She turned back to the counter and slammed the bottle on the countertop. Then she turned back, grabbing the top of my head.

"Lick it up. That's right, like a dog," she yelled at me. "Lick it up—*now.*"

That's when it hit me. At that very moment, it hit me.

Like a dog was all I kept hearing, over and over again in my head. My mind flashed back to when to David was under the kitchen table eating out of the dog dish.

Like a dog—like a dog.

Over and over in my mind, those words just wouldn't stop.

Her hands were forcing my face back onto the floor as I tried to lift my head from the horrid smell. She continued rubbing my face back and forth in the pool of Tabasco as if it were a rag. The pressure from her hand on the back of my head got stronger and stronger.

I closed my eyes tightly. I knew that if I got the Tabasco in my eyes I would really be in trouble. I never opened my mouth. I just let her wipe the floor with my face and shirt.

"Now stand up here," she said.

Once I stood up she pushed me against the refrigerator and grabbed the bottle with her other hand.

"Open up, *now!*" she yelled.

Hesitantly I opened my mouth one last time. Before I realized that she didn't have a spoon in the other hand I felt the top of the glass bottle of Tabasco sauce scrape against my teeth. Once my mouth was full, I had to either swallow it or spit it out. My mistake was to swallow.

"More!"

"More!"

"More!"

A second mouthful went down. That was it. I couldn't take any more.

With tears in my eyes and saliva running out of my mouth, I pushed her hands away and ran out of the kitchen and into the bathroom.

I got sick on the floor and the sink.

Turning to the toilet, I filled my hands with toilet water and brought them up to my mouth as fast as I could before she could stop me. Handful after handful, I washed out as much as I could. My shirt was soaked with Tabasco, spit, and toilet water and smelled worse now than in the kitchen.

"Take that shirt off now!" she said, surprising me.

I froze with fear. She was within striking distance and I had nowhere to run. I expected her to kick and slap me. I tensed all my muscles and held on to the toilet, but nothing happened.

"Take off the shirt, *now!*" she repeated.

Confused that she hadn't hit me, I removed my shirt. Pushing me aside she rinsed the shirt in the bathroom sink and wrung it out.

"Put this back on. *Now!*"

I put on the shirt, wet and still reeking of Tabasco and vomit. As I gathered my schoolbooks and yellow lunch box, she screamed at me to get in the car and sit there until she was ready. I did.

Like a dog was all I could think of. *Like a dog.*

Sitting in the car waiting for her to take me to school, I once again realized that I had become what I'd once loathed. I had become David.

Now I was on my way to setting him up for another fight with Mom. I was about to set David up and give Mom the chance to get him in trouble with the authorities for "stalking" me, as she called it.

As we pulled out of the garage, Mom tossed me another T-shirt. I was ordered to change and toss the dirty one in the backseat of the station wagon.

Once we got to the school we both sat in the office and I waited patiently. Eventually Mom walked me out to the corridors and down the hallway. We eventually reached the spot where I had seen him the day before.

I felt as if I was a convicted prisoner on his way to the electric chair. My head hung low and my *mother* was by my side. As the seconds passed, I heard him call out to me.

"Richard?"

I never looked up. As Mom and I approached him and he approached us, my heart was racing and pounding in my chest. I just couldn't face him.

Don't look at him. Don't look at him, I kept saying to myself.

Once we stopped walking, silence filled the halls. It was as if no one else was there; the halls that contained hundreds of kids a second before were now empty. In reality the halls were full. Kids were walking past and around the three of us, as we just stood there.

I don't recall what Mom said to him. I do recall the tone of her voice. Once again, it was the tone she had used with David when he was in the house. The same tone she now used with me.

When I finally looked up at him it was obvious that she had the same impact on him now that she'd had before. David was completely shocked and horrified to see her.

I looked at him. Once we made eye contact I noticed that David's eyes didn't look through me like before. He was looking into my eyes. The shame and the fear I felt overwhelmed me. He must have known I was the one who'd ratted him out once again by bringing Mom there to torment him.

Before I knew what was happening, David was no longer in sight and Mom was taking me by the arm back to the car.

"That son of a bitch!" she repeated over and over.

"And you—you're dead!" she yelled at me.

As we walked back to the car, her pace quickened as her temper stewed. All I could think was: *He can't help me. He won't help me and now he's gone.*

For so long I was someone who caused David great harm. I was the one who kept him down and lied to Mom about anything he did. I exaggerated everything he did, and didn't do, to keep him in trouble. And now that he'd been freed, I was the one who was down. The one who was afraid. The one that stood in fear, trembling and ashamed to lift my head up.

And just moments before, I'd stood looking at the very one whom I once couldn't understand at all.

Now I understand.

I understand all too well.

At the age of nine, I had gone from predator to prey.

I now fully understood what my older brother was afraid of and why he couldn't sleep at night. I understood why he constantly hung his head down. Not out of shame but out of a sort of twisted respect that Mom commanded.

At some point Mom became convinced that David was out of the Bay Area and living in a jail for kids. She became satisfied that he was finally out of our lives. She was now less afraid of him showing up unexpectedly. But she made certain that I was well aware of the punishment that would follow if I were ever to lay eyes on him again. I was more afraid to see David and have Mom find out than to see David and have him get some sort of revenge on me.

"You'll find yourself in the cell next to him if you open your mouth just once," she would tell me.

As sad as it was, I had to convince myself that David was no longer a brother, he was no longer a thought, he was no longer alive.

Mom's attitude toward me changed after meeting David at school. It changed into a silent treatment, which was fine with me. I knew what the alternative was. Mom and my older brother Scott ran everything in the household. They made decisions as if they were now my parents. They acted responsible for the welfare of what was left of the "family."

Mom seemed to enjoy Scott's authority over me as he commanded that I complete chores he was no longer delegated. I now owned all the dirty and unpleasant chores. I knew I could look forward to each and every unpleasant task the two of them could dream up. Mom always agreed that certain jobs were just right for me. Such as cleaning out the wood cart that sat next to the car in the garage—the same wood cart that I'd slammed my head into years before, the one that hadn't been touched since. The dirt and spiderwebs built up there were horrific. The smells of mold and dust were overpowering. As I cleared out the old logs and the kindling that had never made it to the fireplace, I recalled the face of my older brother living in the basement. I recalled the times I would hide in among the dirt and insects just to get away from Mom.

Past the woodshed on the same side of the garage was the pile of camping gear that also hadn't been touched for years. It was as if the basement was locked in time and nothing had changed. The very place where as a young child I was convinced that time stood still now appeared to have done exactly that. The inches of dust and the cobwebs that stretched across the front of the camping gear reminded me that the basement still held those dark secrets and protected them from anyone else.

The camping gear was stacked more than seven feet high and at least as wide, all tucked neatly in the farthest corner of the basement. I was strictly commanded by Scott to take the collection of gear, place it neatly in the backyard, and wash it all. For hours I cleaned and unpacked years of dirt and dust, shrinking that huge pile to nothing. The backyard's entire cemented area was covered with various items grouped together.

As the day went on and on the work never ended, all I could think about was David and how he'd once slept next to the gear in the basement like an animal that was kept out of sight. I became squeamish as I recalled him, nothing more than some dark secret that was kept barely alive in the basement; he wasn't a brother, or a person, but a thing that lived in the darkness and the cold. Still, I knew that if I didn't focus on the chores at hand, I would wake the demon inside her and once again be at her mercy. I had to clear my mind of David and return to my useless job. I spent most of my time desperately trying to forget him, but seeing the camping gear that I hadn't thought about in years somehow reminded me of him. I'm not sure why, I don't recall him often camping with us, but I did recall him sleeping alone in the corner of the cold basement on that old army cot.

Once I had the pile down to nothing I came across the

old green army cot that had been his bed. That cot I was once so jealous of was now covered with mold and dirt. As I opened it up, I could see the rips and tears in the canvas and I could recall his face once again. I remembered the smell that I associated with him, the sweat and the dirt that lingered in the canvas. That smell was always a part of him. I could see him in my mind lying on the cot in his old and torn gray briefs that should have been tossed out years before. I recalled the times I would become enraged at him just for being alive. It was my place in life to hate him. And now I felt ashamed.

Once I had the gear all arranged and cleaned per Scott's instructions, I let Mom know I was done. She sent Scott down to inspect my work. Time and time again, Scott would find something wrong with what I had done. That provided him the perfect opportunity to rat me out to Mom. Try after try, I worked to get all the gear in order and grouped according to what it was used for. Sleeping bags together next to the cots, cooking gear next to the tools, and so on. After several hours—and then several days— of Scott finding something wrong, and then something else, I built up enough courage to ask Mom directly what she wanted next.

I walked back inside and made my way to the kitchen. I found her just getting off the phone. Taking the only chance I felt I had, I sheepishly asked: "What do you want me to do with the camping gear?"

Annoyed, she walked over to the window behind the dining room table and looked at the organized pile of gear in the backyard.

"I said I want it all thrown out! Everything—it all goes." She walked back into the kitchen.

I knew then that Scott had been playing games with me and wasting all my time and efforts for nothing. It was just his style. He had been taught by the best.

10

CHRISTMAS

*For me, as most of us, Christmas is a favorite time of year.
With the smells and the sounds that fill the air, the holiday
means more to me now than it ever did as a child. The magic
that surrounds Santa Claus is very personal to me. It wasn't
always like that. By the time I was eleven, I knew that Mom
was right, and that even Santa Claus agreed that I was a terrible little redheaded freckle-faced boy who deserved nothing.
Mom had turned me into a subhuman being.*

A T ELEVEN, I found that the best way to judge the
passage of time was by the season of the year. I knew
that summer was here when Mom told me that my birthday
would be another year of: "You're getting nothing."

I knew that winter had arrived when I noticed the early
arrival of dusk and the cold that filled the streets at night as
I walked around them aimlessly and alone. During these
moments of privacy I found the best way to cope with
being lost was to remember better times. Although they
were few and far between, I still had a few special memories

hidden in the archives of my mind. I often think of Christmas now when I reflect.

I recall the one year when Santa must have made two trips for most of the boys in my house.

By now a corner of the basement had been used to build a small room for my older brothers. It took up less than a quarter of the basement. Although it was a hideaway for the older boys, I still felt there the eerie and dark fear that I'd grown to hate in the cellar. It made the walls of that cold chamber of horrors close in.

Each Christmas morning, once all the boys were awake— as if any boy really sleeps on Christmas Eve—my older brothers Ross and Scott would come up from their room and walk carefully into the room Keith and I shared.

Once Mom was awake, and the boys were filled with expectation, Mom would have us line up from youngest to oldest and walk down the long hall to the living room, where Santa had deposited all the presents. Since I was second to the youngest I got the best view in the line. I was taller than my younger brother, Keith, but tall enough to prevent Scott from seeing anything before I could. I never complained about the traditional Christmas-morning lineup.

Once I saw the full-sized pinball machine with the lights flashing and the sounds it made, I knew that Santa had been extra kind this year. I looked around intently for the red ribbon with gold letters that in years past spelled out each of our names attached to the largest gift in the room for each boy. The pinball machine had SCOTT in huge gold letters draped across the top. Carefully placed next to the new Green Machine tricycle was the ribbon with KEITH draped from handle to handle. Across a large pile of electronics was a gold ribbon that said ROSS.

I made my way to the back of the room and looked back. I thought I must have missed my ribbon in all the excitement. But when I scanned the room I found no ribbon that read RICHARD in those gold letters. By now all the other boys were marveling over their piles of gifts and their extra-large presents for being such good kids all year. As I kept looking around, I glanced across at Mom. She nodded toward the bottom of the Christmas tree. I felt relieved that she had noticed I was having trouble finding my pile of wonderful gifts. The first thing I noticed at the bottom of the tree was a ribbon on the floor that read RICHARD. Carefully placed under the ribbon were two comic books.

For a moment I panicked. Had I received nothing? I forced myself to clear my mind and continue to search for my pile of presents. I convinced myself that my ribbon must have fallen off whatever it was attached to. I looked frantically under and anywhere near the tree for my gift. After a moment I came back to that horrible thought I had just a few minutes before: My ribbon on the floor, that gold ribbon that covered the comic books, hid all my presents. I was absolutely crushed.

Secretly all year I had taken comfort in the fact that I would have at least one day of peace and comfort. I believed that the only day of the year I would be allowed to be part of the family was Christmas Day. I looked forward to Christmas as early as March and every day afterward. A whole year of waiting for Santa had now turned into the understanding that Mom had been right all year long.

I looked at Mom and I saw her talking to the other boys about their wonderful gifts. She was telling them how good they must have been all year long and hugged each one of my brothers as he glowed with the joy and excitement of Christmas. I quietly sat on the floor alone and unnoticed.

After a few moments I reached over and picked up the ribbon. I could see one comic book of the Apollo moon landing some ten years before and another of the cartoon character SnagglePuss, who had been on TV years before. I'd always loved the voice and expressions SnagglePuss used when he was on TV.

I picked up the comic books and stared at them. My belief in Santa—the one person who could see that I was really trying to be a good boy and do whatever I was told, and to do it in obedient silence, not complaining about the abuse— simply faded away into obscurity. Even Santa thought I was a terrible child.

I held my comic books close and lay far enough under the tree that I could see the bottoms of all the branches and the colored lights that crisscrossed from branch to branch. I kept crawling backward farther and farther into the corner of the room where the tree stood. Once I was against the wall, I held my comic books against my chest and secretly cried. I could still see the other boys playing with their gifts and looking at each other's presents. Mom was kneeling down talking to Keith. I had been in the corner of the room safely under the tree for fifteen minutes when Mom realized that I had vanished from sight. She looked around for a moment, then walked over to where I was hiding and motioned for me to come closer. I reluctantly obeyed and crawled out from the base of the tree as she leaned over and whispered to me: "If you ruin Christmas for my boys you're going to regret it. Get out from under there and stop crying, *now!*"

When I heard her say "my boys," I knew she was mad.

There were Mom and her boys enjoying the music and the thrill of those few hours before breakfast on Christmas morning, and then there was me. I sat on the floor determined to show no emotion, and I realized what had occurred. Mom had conditioned the rest of the boys to expect that I would be singled out. Just as we all had done to David, when he was living with us. They were conditioned to simply not react.

Once Mom left the room and went into the kitchen to find her bottle, my younger brother, Keith, came over and asked if I wanted to see his new Evel Knievel motorcycle. Before I could sit up, Mom caught me by surprise and grabbed my arm and led me over to the couch. There lay a few presents that had been wrapped without nametags. I had seen them under the tree for weeks but assumed that they were for someone else. The few presents that lay on the couch without names belonged to me.

Usually, each boy would open one present at a time and wait his turn to open another until all the boys had a chance. Eventually, all packages would be opened, and the kids could compare gifts.

I don't recall the contents of my wrapped gifts other than clothes and simple stocking stuffers. I do recall running out of presents to open while the other boys had several more to go as I sat and watched.

I thought about the years before when I was overwhelmed at the amount of presents just for me. I looked at my two comic books and realized that they *were* my gifts. Eventually Keith came back over with the motorcycle. It was a small toy; when it was wound up, it would race down the hallway to crash as it ran out of power. Curious to see what it was, I left my few comic books on the couch and walked over to the hallway. He had set the toy up and was showing me how to run it down the hall.

I glanced over to the kitchen, and at Mom with her glass of vodka. It must have been seven in the morning. Mom had already started her routine as the boys played with their toys. I was just happy to have something and someone to play with, even if it wasn't my toy. We spent what seemed like hours racing the toy down the hallway, and over obstacles we had set up. Keith and I shared a few hours together without Mom interfering.

It was a wonderful time that I will never forget.

Before long, we were told to take the toy outside because Scott needed to move his pinball machine down the hall and into the bedroom where Keith and I slept. Mom was concerned that if the pinball machine was kept in Scott's room, it might keep him up at night, and she didn't want that. Scott was so important to Mom that she made sure that nothing ever made him uncomfortable. Even if it meant that some of the other boys had to give something up.

From the kitchen we heard Mom call out: "Boys—clean up the wrapping paper off the floor and I'll start breakfast."

We all looked forward to Christmas breakfast. Mom always prepared extra food and made a big deal about the table. It was almost as good as opening the presents in years past.

Once we started to gather the wrapping paper into piles, Mom came out of the kitchen, grabbed me by the arm, pulled me into the doorway, and said: "You take the trash down to the basement and wait for me there."

No one seemed to mind having to pick up except me. I was afraid of what Mom wanted me downstairs alone for. Just a few minutes before, Keith and I were having the most fun we'd had with one another in a long time. It was never discussed between us that I had been left off Santa's list of good boys. I guess he'd expected it, where it had caught me by surprise.

Now I was afraid.

Once I took the trash bags of paper down to the basement and placed them near the trash, I stopped and recalled better times. I recalled how excited I used to get over Christmas morning and how my presents made me feel loved. In the middle of my daydream, Mom surprised me as she spun me around to face her in the darkness of the basement— alone.

I panicked when she leaned in close to me and glared at me with her red and swollen eyes. "I bought those books for you," she said. "The only reason I did was so that you wouldn't make a scene while my boys open their gifts. There is no Santa Claus and it's time you understood that. I am the only one who takes care of this family and you."

I had heard from other kids that the magic of Christmas and Santa Claus was brought to life by the love of a parent, but never wanted to believe it. Now I knew.

Mom had taken from me the last piece of childhood I had left. She took from me the belief in the magic and that special hope that only Santa can keep alive.

Mom smiled as she turned and walked away. Alone and in the darkness of the basement I sat and cried.

Before long, morning had turned into afternoon and Mom had started the elaborate Christmas dinner. As I sat on the couch in the front room I was able to quietly take in my surroundings. Mom had always enjoyed decorating the house top to bottom from Halloween to New Year's Day. The front room, where the tree stood, was filled with holiday decorations. The fireplace mantel held ornaments and lights, as did everything in the room. It was magical. I sat and recalled a few years before when I'd jumped up and down as I saw my red ribbon with gold letters draped across the handlebars of a new bicycle. I recalled riding the bike just a few feet down the driveway and how I was afraid that the training wheels would fall off and I would crash. All the simple memories of better times came back to me, and I understood that those days were gone.

I stood up from the concrete floor and walked over to where David had once slept near the back of the base- ment. As I stood looking at the empty place where the green army cot used to stand, I cried. I knew at that mo- ment that I had become like him. Different and yet the same. I wasn't part of the family, and I wasn't part of any- thing else. I was alone and I was hurt. I wondered what David must have thought about when he had a few min- utes alone in the basement to think. I wondered if he had thought of better times or if he didn't have any better memories to recall. I closed my eyes and walked back to the steps that led to the upstairs and the front room, filled with music and the noise of toys and my brothers' laugh- ter. Quietly I walked up the steps and into my room and climbed into the upper bunk—alone.

Dinner was ready before long and I didn't feel belittled by the normal routine of having to wait for my younger brother to start eating, then finish before he did. The table looked as if it was set for a king. Tall red candles that sat on the buffet—some of them were two feet high—and little figurines scattered in cotton as if it was snow were just a few of the decorations visible to me. As dinner was set on the table, the record player in the front room softly played Harry Belafonte, Nat King Cole, and, of course, Bing Crosby. It was worth the entire year of hell just to have a few hours of peace between Mom and me. These memories of Christmas are without a doubt the best memories I have.

Once nightfall came and Christmas Day was nearing its close, each boy would usually sit near the tree and marvel at his gifts. I was comfortable just lying under the tree and looking up at the colored lights as they flickered in the dark. I sat there for hours, warm and satisfied that, even if it was only one day, I enjoyed it.

One of the few times any relative dared to stay in the house for more than a few minutes was Christmas. Grandma had come out from Salt Lake City, Utah, to spend a couple of days with us.

When we found out that Gram was coming out, just before the holidays, Mom carefully coached me on what to say and definitely on what *not* to say. Ross and Scott got the message the first time and apparently did not need to be told as often as I did. Mom would rehearse me in all the things I should say and make sure she was comfortable with my tone and my delivery. She made sure that I was mean and cold to Gram in anything I was taught to repeat. Mom was very careful to let Gram know that she was in no way any part of Mom's life. I was coached to say such things as:

"This is our family Christmas. Why are you here?"

"These things are for family only, and you're not family."

I knew that speaking to an adult with any sort of disrespect, or telling lies, was completely unacceptable, except when it came to Gram. I was not only allowed to, but also encouraged to treat Gram like a second-rate human. Since I had more than my share of it myself, I was comfortable enough in dishing it out. Mom had prepared each of the boys for Grandma's arrival with a repeated long speech about how she might "try to take over Christmas and ruin it for all of us. Don't let her get involved in our family. These events are for family only."

Mom had no second thoughts about telling her own mother that she wasn't invited. She told her own mother that she was "nonexistent." Several times Mom told Gram on the phone that she wasn't welcome and wasn't part of her family. Most of the time that happened during one of her drunken stupors, her evil personality showing through. It always amazed me that Mom had such a hatred for her mother; not that I didn't have hatred for my own. I often wondered how Grandma dealt with knowing that her daughter was a severe alcoholic and one of the most abusive parents in history. Grandma seemed to hold it all in. At least it didn't show on the surface.

Perhaps Gram knew more about her daughter's mental state than she let on. They got along like cat and mouse: One of them was always after the other for one thing or another. Mom convinced me that that Gram was an old, evil person who would ruin our family if we let her.

I recall Gram sitting near the large bay window and watching the kids play in the front room. I approached her with my rehearsed speech.

"You're not welcome in our family. You should go back to your home," I commanded.

I had delivered my rehearsed torment and returned to the kitchen. Mom was happy that I was able to complete the task she had given me with such finesse. She smiled and reassured me I had done well.

With that, Gram was packed and out of the house before breakfast, driving back home, alone. I had known full well the real hurt I had caused. I didn't feel sorry for her. If Gram really knew that her daughter was mentally ill and completely unstable, she should have ensured that the authorities took the rest of the children.

This was the struggle between mother and daughter, Mom and Grandma. They both couldn't, or perhaps wouldn't, see the damage being done to each other; nor did they care. They each had their own concerns. Each looked out only for herself.

The relationship between the kids growing up and Gram can only be described as phony, at least from my perspective. I never knew if the other boys were able to get past the bitterness between Mom and Gram and see Gram for who she really was. In later years I learned that Gram was a kind but demanding person. She had little room in her heart for people who hurt her or treated her poorly. Mom had been treating Gram with unmerciful cruelty for years.

Now, in addition to being the recipient of miserable family relationships, I was contributing to the building of hatred and mistrust. Once again, I was the pawn and Mom was controlling me. It took several years to understand what she was doing and how she would adjust her tactics in using the kids to advance her personal needs. She never hesitated to crush my self-esteem or any pride I was able to muster, no matter how short-lived it was.

11

A CRACK IN THE ICE

My youth and my inexperience at dealing with someone as deranged as my mother didn't prevent me from trying to understand what was happening to me. I had resolved to find a way to stop her. I was sure that if I found something that she was afraid of, that I could use against her, it would stop the madness. At the age of eleven I thought I had found a crack in her armor. I thought I had found a crack in the ice.

THE END OF THE 1976 school year came as expected; uneventful. My last day at elementary school, at eleven, I experienced my biggest disappointment yet. As usual, I was called down to the principal's office to sit in the lobby one last time. I could never understand why it was so important for the principal to know the details about my life. School was the one place where I had the slightest confidence that I could find a saving grace. But by the time I left elementary school I had a different view of the school and the staff.

Mom had told me that they might pry and try to trip me up in anything I said. She told me: "Watch what you say and tell me everything they ask you. They might try to send you to jail, like David, if they know how bad you are. So don't say anything."

I was afraid to talk to the office lady and terrified to talk to the principal in private. Inside, I hoped and prayed that the principal would somehow learn of the real horrors that went on in my house and step in. In the back of my mind, I wondered if the school was really looking out for me or just "out to get me," as Mom would say during one of her many lectures. I had been in the office so many times and nothing was ever said or done.

By the last day of school, I barely held on to the expectation that each day might be my day of deliverance. Each walk from the office and back to the classroom destroyed a bit more of my faith that I might be rescued someday. As I sat waiting for the principal I prayed that today would be the day that I would receive word of help.

Hours before, back in the classroom, the children had been talking about what they wanted to be when they grew up. *Firemen, teachers,* and *astronauts* were the kinds of answers most of the kids gave. Terrified of speaking in class, I was happy to hear the phone ring to call me down to the office once again. I knew that if I'd had to say something, I would have only stuttered and looked stupid again in front of the class.

Before long I could hear the principal as she walked out of her office. She was speaking about the different responses the children gave in the classroom she had visited earlier. When she saw me sitting on the couch, the expression on her face told me that she had forgotten that I was there. She came over and sat down next to me. With a smile she asked, "What do you want to be when you grow up?" She seemed to have a true sense of curiosity.

I simply answered: "A kid!"

As the look on her face changed from happy to serious, she compassionately asked again what I really wanted to be.

I couldn't think of an answer. I couldn't find anything within myself that allowed me to think about my future. I had been living day-to-day for so long that it actually took me by surprise that anyone would ask the question. As the silence filled the room, the tension became overpowering. I looked deep inside myself for an honest answer, but a familiar emptiness was all I found. The emptiness had been there for years, growing larger and larger each time I was told I was worthless and had no place in life.

With her arms across my shoulder, the principal asked: "A policeman?"

"Maybe," I replied, as if I was asking her permission.

I found it odd that the one thing she suggested was the one thing I could never be. I had grown to fear the police, even more so after Mom's wrath at my being seen with a police officer. It was the last thing I had ever expected the principal to say. Without hesitation, I accepted her suggestion and made believe I was enthusiastic about it. But I knew in my heart that I would never amount to anything like that. I knew I would never become someone who was looked up to or respected. In an attempt to repay her for all the kindness she had shown me over the years, I made it a point to show my appreciation for her vote of confidence and to appear to be happy. With that, she stood up, walked over to the secretary's desk, and announced that I was going to be a policeman. After a moment she excused me to return to class.

As I went back to class, I knew there wasn't going to be any help from the school. Angry at the thought of being left alone again, I saw no reason to go back to class. The confusion between the great need to keep the secret and the need to ask for help simply added to my sense of failure.

Why should I go back?

So I can get ridiculed or laughed at?

Perhaps I would enjoy the hollow laughter of the final day. Hollow in the sense that I was so empty inside and the kids seemed to enjoy the festivities. All I could relate their laughter to was the emptiness I knew when they laughed at me, behind my back and to my face. I wanted no part of their happiness. I knew then that no one would do anything about my home or my mom. I was simply stuck with the life I had. At the age of eleven, I had to accept my environment. I prayed that I would eventually shrink so small that I would just evaporate into nothingness. I talked myself into closing up so tight that no one would ever get through to me.

I was disappointed and angered by the way I was simply shuffled out of elementary school and into middle school. All my hopes, all my prayers of the school saving me melted into that place in my heart that held all the tears that never made it to my face. Only now that place was full.

At that moment, I knew I was completely on my own. I felt like a helpless child, powerless to do anything about my situation. I couldn't find anything inside to be happy about or proud of; not even the slightest bit of good about myself.

I convinced myself to bury every form of expression and emotion. I just couldn't take any more disappointments.

———

Many of my memories for the next several months and even years are buried so deep that I find it difficult to recall anything after that. I shut down emotionally. Summer came and went with the usual doses of punishments and new lessons to learn. The ongoing private lessons that kept me "in check" had less impact than those lessons of prior years. I just didn't care anymore. I cried less and less. Though the pain was always just as hurtful as before, it now didn't faze me. I was completely shut down and void of emotion. The only difference in my routine during that summer was the Bicentennial celebration that I was permitted to watch on television from time to time.

When I was younger, I had felt sorry for my brothers and myself. By the time that summer ended, I couldn't even feel self-pity. I simply felt nothing. Mom had little effect on me, and I accepted everything she had to dish out. I found no motivation for maintaining the collection of junk in my room to update the defense on which I'd been so dependent. I had no desire to run from Mom in the mornings or yell back at her when I knew she was wrong about something I did or didn't do. It was as if I went through the whole summer in a sort of dream. I can't recall any memories of Josh or his brother, Kevin, that summer, no vacations, no camping, no brothers or anything else.

For most kids, I would imagine that moving from grammar school to middle school would be an exciting time. It would mean changing from having the same teachers all day to having scheduled classes in different rooms and different periods. It would mean walking on your own from one class to another, and to the all-important cafeteria. For years I had dreamed of what it would be like.

Now that it was here, I felt nothing. The excitement was absent. It wasn't until the third or fourth week of school that I mustered up enough courage to ask Mom to purchase a set of gym sweats, which I was required to have for P.E. I had to have them by the following Monday or I wouldn't be allowed to take the class and would lose credit. All weekend I tried to find a way to ask her without creating another reason for her to teach me a lesson. I hid the notice I had received at school in my pocket. I knew it was safe there. I'd been doing my own laundry for years.

That Saturday night I decided to break the news that I wouldn't pass gym if I didn't have the proper clothes by Monday. Shortly after dinner was over and the dish chores were done, I walked around the house to find Mom. I knew she would explode at the news that I needed something from her, but I had no choice. If I didn't get the clothes, I would fail gym, and she would have justification to punish me.

As I walked past the downstairs door, I could hear the voice I had come to loathe. I knew she was on her way upstairs and would see me standing at the top of the steps looking like a sick puppy. With no desire to try to anticipate her reaction, as I simply didn't care anymore, I waited at the top of the steps.

"What the hell is wrong with you?" she barked out as she neared the top of the steps. Before I even began my stuttered replies she told me: "Get out of my sight until you can learn to speak clearly."

She never even gave me the chance to open my mouth— she knew all too well that I would stutter and look stupid. She simply showed me her disgust and walked away.

Past caring, I stuck my chin into my chest and walked to my room. Shortly after, as I sat on the desk looking out the window, she came into the room again.

"What the hell's wrong with you?" she demanded.

I jumped off the desk, stood just a few feet away from her, and broke the news. I finished by adding that the teacher had made it clear that I must have the clothes. She simply said "No!" and walked away.

It could have been worse, I guess, I thought.

I went back to the desk and looked out the window. I didn't care either way. Once the streetlights came on and the kids began to disappear from the street, I climbed to the upper bunk and got under the covers.

The night was clear, and the smell of the fog and dampness filled the air. One of the few things I enjoyed in Daly

City was that smell. I decided that if I opened the window a little more, I could enjoy the quiet and perhaps see a few stars. Grabbing the end of the sheets tucked tightly around my head, I pulled them off to lean over to the window at the foot of the bed.

She was there. She was right there!

I saw her face just inches away from my head. She had been standing motionless, not making a sound, waiting for me to move. I didn't know what else to do, so I grabbed the sheets as if I was going to cover my head again and hide as I had done many times before. Before I could make it under the covers, she ripped them out of my hands and pushed my head back toward the mattress. I had sat up when I uncovered my head and I was now sitting on my pillow. With the force of her push I fell backward and over the headboard, which is just a few inches taller than the pillow, and down to the floor from the top bunk. Without wasting any time she began to yell at me for the problem I had caused her by making her buy the gym clothes I needed. Once I could see where she was I put my hand on the floor to push myself up to my knees. A sharp pain shot from my wrist deep into my arm. Favoring that hand, I allowed myself to fall back to the floor and onto my side. Before I hit the floor, she kicked me in the side and I slid into the orange dresser next to my bunk bed. The force of her kick caused the dresser to rock back and forth just enough to push off the record player I kept on top. It fell onto my head and shoulder as I lay below it. The sound and the crash scared me more than the pain it caused. Unexpectedly, Mom started laughing at me with a deep belly laugh, as if this was one of the funniest things she had ever seen. She laughed louder and louder, pointing down at me as I sat on the floor rubbing my head and shoulder. I saw the record player in pieces on the hardwood floor. The combination of that laugh of hers and the sight of my record player broken fueled the eruption of the emotions I had hidden away all summer. I had been angry before and had managed to hold it in. I thought that if I was ever to let it all go, it would be after a long struggle to hold back until I just couldn't hold back anymore.

I lifted my face up and looked her straight in the eye and said: "You bitch!"

I knew that what I'd said would cause the gates of Hell to open, and the wrath of Mom to be unleashed, but I didn't care. As she bent down to my level on the floor she grabbed both my ears to hold my face in front of hers.

"Just get one thing straight, mister—you're all mine, and I can kill you anytime I want."

Her tone was serious, and her eyes were bloodshot. I couldn't tell if it was from the vodka or her anger, but I knew that she meant what she said. I was afraid. I was very afraid.

After a second of staring at each other, and me frozen with fear, she spit in my face, shoved my head back into the dresser, and casually walked out of the room.

I remember sitting in that same spot for a while thinking. I couldn't believe what I had said. I was shocked at the ease with which I'd let my thoughts out of my mouth. I couldn't decide whether I had made a mistake or finally found the guts to fight back. Perhaps I had; perhaps I would be able to stand up to her. Almost with a sense of pride, I carefully climbed back to the upper bunk and got back under the covers. In an odd sort of way I slept soundly that night. Somehow I knew that she wouldn't be back.

Sunday came and went without incident. Mom actually ignored me the entire day, which was fine with me. At some point during the day she took my other brothers out to Westgate Shopping Center and returned with a green sweat suit with a white stripe down the legs and sleeves. She walked into my room, tossed the sweats on the floor, and without saying a word walked back out. I marveled at the event. I had actually gotten what I needed, and all I had had to do was stand up to her. I knew that I had discovered a flaw in her I hadn't seen before. Perhaps I had missed something critical in the past. From that point forward I had a weapon, a means to fight back. I had a ray of hope.

Over the next few weeks I began mouthing back to her every chance I could. Louder, and longer, I would attempt to express my true feelings. Between stuttering and being completely frightened, I would yell whatever I felt. More often than not Mom would back down, usually because my other brothers would come into the room to find out what the yelling was all about. With that revelation, I discovered that part of Mom's power over me was the fact that she would carefully plan to have the other boys downstairs or outside when she unloaded on me. Now I knew that all I had to do was make such a commotion that Mom would have to back down. I couldn't believe I had missed that one crucial piece of knowledge. I guess I had been so wrapped up in just trying to survive that I had overlooked the simplest and most effective means of survival. Taking away her ability to continue the abuse was all I needed to do. It was odd to realize that the one thing I feared the most—speaking out and letting our little secret be exposed—was the one thing that could stop it all.

Mom knew exactly what she was doing by instilling the years and years of fear. She was a master at fear. With my new knowledge, I developed a strength I didn't have before. For the first time, I could stand up and be noticed as a human being and a real person inside our house.

As the weeks passed, and we played our little games, I had no hesitation in screaming at the top of my lungs whenever she came close to me. The sense of power it gave me was incredible. More important, I discovered that Mom was hollow inside and worthless to me. She was nothing more than a miserable part of my fading childhood. For the first time in my life I had won. It seemed as if I had control over her now, and I was going to use it.

Or so I thought.

One Friday, as I came home from school, I looked over the fence into the backyard and saw my precious boomerang table, the black lacquer stereo cabinet, and all the pieces of furniture I had collected over the years for the middle of my room. They were all broken into small scraps and piled up in the backyard. I went directly into my room and found everything cleaned out. There was nothing I could see that I could call my own. My orange dresser, the books on the black desk, the furniture, the fish tank on the long table—they were all gone. I was shocked. I'd never thought she could or would destroy the few possessions I had, even if they were junk. I just couldn't believe it.

I opened the sliding door to the closet and found it nearly empty. Mom had spent the day destroying and throwing out anything that I had held on to; anything that even reminded her of me. My clothes were now in the old dresser hidden in the closet, and there was nothing else to be seen that I could call my own, other than the bunk bed. As I turned around to look under the bed for anything she'd left, I noticed Mom standing in the doorway, leaning against the wall, cracking a smile.

"You just won't learn, will you—you can't win." With that, she turned to leave.

"You want to play games, I'll play games!" I coldly said. "I can play games you don't even know about. We can play—who wants to talk to the police? You bitch!"

She was walking away, but she abruptly stopped in her tracks and looked back at me, confusion coming over her. At the same time I realized that I had spoken in a clear and deep voice. I hadn't stuttered a single word. It was as if I was someone else, and it made me feel that I had the upper hand. Now she was the one who was in the dark, wondering what would happen next. In a way, I had a victory, small but significant.

For the last several years I had been storing certain memories of Mom's flaws to evaluate later and find some small weakness I could use. This latest show of my attitude was the biggest breakthrough yet. Over the next few weeks I put together a pattern of what Mom was doing. I began to understand who she was. Even though I was only eleven, I began to try to understand Mom. I tried to figure her out and find what made her who she was. I had to find out.

Over time I realized that she was unhappy about being a parent. She seemed to resent having the responsibility of children, almost as if it took too much time away from her. With Dad out of the house, she had no outlet for her twisted emotions. I believed that she turned to my older brother as an out when things with Dad went wrong. After David was taken out of the house by the state, Mom continued her abuse, only in a slightly different manner. She was more careful in her actions, more personal in her approach, always careful to hide the secret not only from the world but also from other members of her family. I began to understand that she needed the release of letting out her anger. I could understand the need to let it all out. For years I had been carrying around feelings and fears that now were surfacing in a volcano.

Perhaps Mom and I needed the same things, only she couldn't find a way to deal with it. Perhaps she and I had something in common after all—common needs that almost fed off each other. Now that I could understand Mom a little bit better, I discovered an emotion that had been hidden for many years: pity.

After all, she was my mom and was seriously mentally ill. That was obvious to anyone, even to a boy like me. I knew I had to be careful. I had made the mistake of trying to get into her head and outsmart her many times before, and I had failed. This time I knew what I had to do.

I had to bury my feelings deeper than ever before. I had to ignore that strange sense of pity and love for Mom, I had to ignore that still small voice that came to me from time to time, I had to remember that we were the same, Mom and me—only different. We were opposite sides of the same coin. We were enemies.

I had to stand up to her. I had finally found a crack in the ice I had been looking for. I wasn't about to lose the chance to break free, not now.

12

FULL CIRCLE

Despite winning some small battles, by the time I turned twelve I knew that I was incapable of stopping Mom. She had years of experience at masking the truth to anyone who dared to ask. I had thought a lot about what I had done to my older brother years before and was beginning to understand him. My life had evolved into the very life that David once suffered. I had become his replacement. In an odd sort of way, I thought it justice for those years of hell I caused him. My life had now gone full circle. I had become what I once loathed.

ONCE I STARTED TO ADJUST to the change from elementary school to middle school, I found that, with the larger number of students in both the classrooms and the school as a whole, I easily fit into a sort of social void. Although I had no social circle to speak of, I was in a crowd of other kids anywhere I went. From the lunchroom to the courtyard, among hundreds of kids I managed to be alone in the middle of the crowd.

It didn't take long before I was identified as a "loner," and often "weird." The comments were similar to what I was used to, but they hurt me more than ever before. I guess I'd sort of expected the cruelty of kids to fade away as we all grew older and moved up to the middle school level. This, too, was just another futile hope. I found the kids in my new surroundings to be more cruel and threatening than I'd ever anticipated.

Once the kids formed their own cliques and groups in and out of the classrooms, it became obvious that I was an outsider. I found myself in the library seeking shelter from the world as often as time would allow. Fortunately the library was much larger than the one at the elementary school. Unfortunately, I was not accepted there as well as in elementary school, where I was sort of looked after by the staff. Here no one really noticed just another shy and awkward student— many other students were experiencing the same awkwardness and took refuge in the library just like me.

After the first month of the school year I knew that I must either make it clear that I wouldn't stand for being one of the crowd's targets or simply accept my place and try to deal with it. The inevitable day came—the day when I found myself deciding which direction I would take. A big, overweight kid made it a point to mock me as I walked by his small group of friends at one of the round tables in the library. As silence filled the room, I built up the courage to come up with a response. All that I could think of was simply, "Go to hell!"

It was a phrase that I was more than used to at home. Whenever I asked for something or needed help with my schoolwork, it was all I ever heard. Within moments the big kid was up out of his seat and in my face cursing at me. As he realized that the other students were watching, he must have felt the need to hold his ground, just as I did. With a quick and forceful shove he pinned me to the floor. Weighing considerably more than I, he had me on the ground nearly unable to defend myself. As his fist struck me time and time again, I felt the same anger against my mother, against my life erupt to the surface. I launched a fist into his jaw. Surprisingly, the force knocked him off me, and I was now free to defend myself. The other students were just as amazed as I was. Before either of us could think of anything else, the staff in the library came over, took each of us by the arm, and walked us down to the main office. There, I realized that I had put myself in jeopardy—I'd given Mom another excuse to unload on me.

As I sat outside the seventh-grade counselor's office, the door opened and I was summoned inside. The man behind the desk was clear in his tone and made it obvious that he was upset with me. I was informed that my parents had been asked to come and pick me up from school, and that I was being suspended. Emotionlessly, I simply asked if my mom was coming to pick me up.

"Yes, I spoke to her a few minutes ago," I was told.

I guess I was expecting an opportunity to bare my feelings to an adult and be able to share what I had been going through. I was used to this kind of treatment—counselors or the principal talking to me about my feelings and how things were going at home. Without a single opportunity to say anything, I was simply informed of the school policy and told that I had broken it. As the counselor spoke I realized that I had, again, reverted to placing my chin into my chest and hanging my head down while being spoken to. Once I was aware of my body language I felt like I was in front of Mom being yelled at for something that I didn't do.

In a sharp voice, he ordered me to remain in the hallway until Mom arrived and signed me out of school. I knew she wouldn't be there right away. Mom needed time to get herself together, and that would take a while. Before the second bell rang, the father of the student I had fought with came in and picked him up. He scowled at me, as though I was to blame for his son's behavior. Before long the third bell of the day rang; the counselor came out and noted that I was still awaiting Mom's arrival. As the time passed, I tried to think of things that took my mind off Mom and what was awaiting me at home. I thought of the backyard and the hill where I would play with Matchbox cars and the peace and quiet it afforded me. Shortly the fourth bell rang and first-period lunch started. Again the counselor came out and saw me sitting as before. Try as I might, I just couldn't take my mind off what Mom would do to me the second she got me home. Again a bell rang. Second lunch started.

Shortly after the fifth bell the counselor came out and informed me that he had called my house again with no answer.

"It shouldn't be much longer now. I guess she is on her way," he said.

He walked back inside the office. Startled at the sound of the sixth bell, I realized that I had drifted off and fallen asleep in the chair. Once I regained my composure, I was summoned over to the secretary's desk and asked to call my house from her phone. I reluctantly walked over to her desk. The lump in my throat seemed to grow as I heard the first and second ring of the phone. I finally said: "Hello, Mom?"

Before I could get another word in she yelled loud enough that the secretary looked up.

"What the hell have you done now? If you think I'm going to drive down there and pick up your miserable butt, you're crazy as hell."

As Mom continued to blast me, it became apparent that the secretary was able to hear her. I placed the receiver closer to my ear and pretended that I was allowed to speak. Without breaking stride Mom continued to unleash her verbal abuse.

"You're on your way now?" I said.

"What? Did you hear me; you're on your own, mister."

"Okay, I'll see you in a while," I calmly said.

Both the secretary and I could hear Mom yelling even louder through the phone as the receiver touched the cradle and silence filled the air. Without a word I walked back to my seat and slumped down as before.

The seventh and final bell rang for the day, and my counselor came out and told me that I'd have to walk home and deliver a letter to my parents myself. He handed me the envelope. I stood up and went out to the courtyard for my walk home.

I knew that Mom had no intention of picking me up and would have had plenty of time to stew over my disruption of her day. As I walked home, I prepared myself for whatever she could come up with this time. I tried thinking of places where I wasn't afraid; the backyard came to mind, and I enjoyed reflecting on the peace and quiet I found there. Before long I was standing at the bottom of Crestline Avenue looking up the street. I could see Mom's car parked there just as it had been when I'd walked to school that morning.

Once I was close enough to the house I could feel in the pit of my stomach the all-too-familiar fear. The predictable reaction Mom would have as she saw me enter the house was what I feared most. Standing at the bottom of the front steps, I gathered my thoughts, then walked up to the top and reached for the door. Before I could touch the doorknob she opened the door.

"Get your butt in here—right now," she demanded.

I entered the front room and could see Scott sitting at the dining room table. Once he saw me he stood up and went into the kitchen where Mom now was.

"What the hell do you think you're doing? You deliberately hung up on me when I was talking to you!" she shouted.

Scott made eye contact with me as he asked: "Do you know how disrespectful that is?"

I knew Scott and Mom had already talked about what happened to me at school today and had probably agreed on some sort of twisted punishment.

In a pointless attempt to calm her down, I deliberately favored my right hand while we talked. Eventually Scott asked: "What's wrong with your hand?"

Without a glance at Scott, I looked at Mom and said: "I think it's broken. It hurts from hitting that boy at school."

It was only an attempt to change the subject and see if she would show any sort of motherly concern. Would one of my newly developed strategies work or would she give in to her need to lash out?

Carefully she said: "Step over here and show me your hand."

Hoping for sympathy, I did as she commanded. After a short inspection, my brother came over to have a look. I pulled my hand away and down to my side. Mom and Scott looked at each other, and almost as if they had rehearsed prior to my arrival, Mom walked over to the pantry door in the kitchen and summoned me over.

"Hold this," she said.

She pointed to the side of the pantry doorjamb just above the brass plate where the door latch caught when it closed. I did as she commanded and listened to Scott repeat what he had said just a few minutes before: "You need to learn respect!"

Within a flash I realized that I had been set up again. As I turned my head from Scott back to Mom I could see Mom's face turn angry as she forcefully swung the door closed. Not thinking fast enough, I failed to pull my hand out of the doorjamb, and the door slammed into the back of my palm. As the pain screamed up my arm from what seemed like every bone in my hand, I could hear Scott again: "Learn respect for your mother and me."

The door bounced back open and I pulled my hand out of it, but Mom reached out and caught the door to swing it shut again.

"Now, get your butt downstairs. I'll be down in a minute!" she screamed.

I hadn't realized it, but that moment was the first time in a long time that she'd wanted me downstairs during one of our little sessions. It was also the first time that Mom had done anything to me with someone else in the room. The previous summer, I had learned that she wouldn't do anything to me if someone else was watching. The fact that she had now yelled at me in front of Scott and had in some way made him part of her plan made me realize that she had turned another dangerous corner.

Once I made it to the bottom landing of the downstairs steps, I held my hand and looked around to hide. The basement was cold and dark. Silence filled the room as I went around to the back of the garage and the backyard door. I could see where David had once slept.

As the thought of David came to mind, I realized what she had done. She had successfully put me in the one place I never wanted to be alone with her. It was the place I feared the most; the basement and the cold concrete walls provided the privacy and security she needed. As I stood there alone with one hand in the other, I looked for an answer. My attention turned to the back door and the backyard where I had been, mentally, most of the afternoon. I moved carefully to the bottom of the steps and listened for any sign of Mom or Scott. In silence I turned and went to the back door. As I reached out to turn the knob I could feel the pain in my wrist and hand. Switching hands, I opened the door and ran to the hill at the back part of the yard. There, on the left portion of the yard along the fence where our neighbors Tony and Alice lived, was a large area of pampas grass. The bushes were nearly six feet high and just as wide and offered a perfect place to crawl in and hide.

I had been in the bushes years before to retrieve balls, but I'd never been in them to hide. I found out the hard way that pampas grass is not the best place to seek shelter. The leaves of the bushes were long and thin and had sharp edges. Since the leaves were taller than I was, it was difficult to move them out of the way without getting cut. But I had committed myself to going in and hiding in the bushes, and I had to get in as far as I could. Before long I had cut my arms and hands badly. Eventually I found a place where I could fold the leaves one on top of another and make a sort of seat to sit on. Once I found the most comfortable spot, I sat waiting for Scott to come into the backyard looking for me.

As I sat, I thought about David and how I had become his worst enemy by turning on him as instructed by Mom. Now it had come full circle. My brother had turned on me, and I was unable to do anything about it. In an odd way, I felt as if it was some sort of justice for all the times I had ratted David out. As I thought about the many times I had betrayed my brother, I understood Mom even more. It became obvious that she needed the people around her to provide support for her insanity.

With the years flashing through my mind, I fell asleep in my new hiding place.

When I opened my eyes, darkness surrounded me. I had been in the grass far longer than I had planned. Only the front yards of the houses on my street were lit. The backyards were dark and terrifying to a kid at night. Once I recalled what had happened that afternoon, I found my way out of the grass and to the opening of the backyard. I was covered with insects and dirt. I brushed myself off as best I could and climbed back to the top of the hill. Looking up into the large windows in the back of the house, I could see that the lights in the living room and dining room were still on. I had no idea of the time as I opened the back door and went into the garage.

At the top of the steps that led to the kitchen I saw Mom sitting at the table with her back toward me, drinking from that same gray glass of vodka. I simply slipped by unnoticed and went into my room. The need for a bath was not as important as the need to remain invisible.

I'll try to sneak a shower in the morning, I thought.

13

SAYING GOOD-BYE
TO MY HERO

Ross was the oldest and the most handsome of my brothers.
Many times he was my protector, and he was always my
hero. Ross was eighteen and I was only twelve, but he sel-
dom excluded me from his life. Often he allowed me to
spend time with him and his much older friends. I loved to
ride with him in his magnificent Dodge Polara ex–police
car. I should have known that he would take the first chance
he had to get out of that house of madness. I just wish I
could have said good-bye to him the way I wanted to—like
brothers.

THE SUMMER OF 1977 brought many unexpected
changes. My world opened a little wider, and I became
aware of life as a person. My friend Josh, across the street, had
a sister named Donna. Donna was a very cute girl who
seemed to like Ross and me. I always knew she had a crush
on Ross, and that was all right with me. I was just happy that

I had a friend. Donna was always very interested in being around my oldest brother. When we had time to be together outside the house, it was like another world for me. I was able to watch and experience other kids as we played together.

Bike riding was the best time we had that summer. I was allowed to go beyond my former boundary limit of Crestline Avenue and seek new roads and adventures on other streets. Not that we brothers hadn't done it before, behind Mom's back, but now it was official; I had permission.

It was amazing to realize that kids I had seen in school for years lived only a few blocks away. Some were even on the next street. Now I had a bike and the permission to venture onto their turf to see them as if I was observing creatures in their habitats. The possibilities seemed endless: to be able to travel at will from Westmore Avenue down to the corner of Ocean Grove, down Beechwood Road, up to Montrose Avenue, and back to Southgate Avenue. The world was opening up to me in ways I couldn't understand at the time.

Life became more daring than it had been—inside and outside the house. Josh and I thought of new ways to have fun and create adventures, like roller-skating from one end of Ocean Grove to the other.

It seemed to me that the more I grew up outside the house, the more I learned new things in the house. There were new cruel games to be played out behind closed doors between Mom and me. Mom came up with new punishments for the growing boy who was supposed to be so violent and dangerous. She had started to use food as a sort of reward for me. She always kept the kitchen pantry full of Craigmont soda for the kids. My favorite was the cream soda. I always had a supply; none of the other boys liked it. But now Mom made sure that I couldn't have any. The other boys would be able to run in the house and grab a few sodas and run back outside to play. Mom kept count of the number of cream soda cans and would punish me for taking any. Up to this point she had never singled me out when it came to food. Sure, I was made to feel like a second-rate person at the dining table when I had to wait for my younger brother to start eating and had to finish before he did. But the food was always great and always more than enough. Now it was as if I had to earn drinks and snacks, though none of the other boys did.

As I grew, I became part of something unexpected: More and more, I was asked to tag along and go somewhere with Ross and some of his friends. I always wondered whether it was a result of Mom's instructions or my brother's desire. Ross was so easy to talk to and easy to listen to. Whenever I became too talkative, which was most of the time, a simple glance from Ross would shut me up. By this time, my stuttering had faded away. I only stuttered around Mom or any adult whom I was frightened of.

Just being around Ross made me so proud, so happy, and so comfortable. I would do anything at all to keep that faith and that trust.

When I was called onto Ross's team for football games, I always felt good. It was also great for a laugh or two. My brother and his friends towered over me by at least two feet. There was no way I could contribute to the efforts of the team. Just seeing me try to be open for the pass, or to guard the kid three feet taller than I was so he couldn't catch the ball, must have been comical. For me, just being there was happiness; being wanted was more than I could ever ask. It was always made clear to me that I was truly a third wheel and subject to dismissal at any time, but that was okay with me. I always tried not to damage my brother's image or embarrass him.

Some of the best memories I had with Ross were with a friend of his named Brad, and of Brad's baby blue Cougar with wide rear tires and a loud stereo system. A white interior and a large eight-ball for the shift handle made this baby one of the coolest cars in the neighborhood.

Brad was always good for upsetting Mom when he would stop right in front of the house, rev the motor, and pop the clutch to release the popular burning rubber smoke that seemed to fill the whole block. The smell and the sounds were incredible. It was so cool that he could do that—and even better that it seemed to be directed at Mom. Even if it wasn't, I thought so, and that was good enough for me. Someone was actually standing up to her and there was nothing she could do about it.

Or so I thought.

The one big argument between my hero and Mom resulted in a long drawn-out verbal battle, which he lost. As if he truly thought he could win. He was officially banned from having "that boy and his car around my house," she said.

I felt so bad for Ross that I wanted to stop her by deliberately doing something wrong to spare Ross. I hoped that she would forget about him for the moment and he would be off the hook. Thinking quickly, I smacked my younger brother, Keith, on the back of the head and he screamed. Hurting my younger brother was always good for a serious beating or severely long punishment. He was too young to be part of my hero's band of friends. He was too young to be part of anything, really; he just didn't fit in because of his age. As I expected, she came flying out of the kitchen and started in on me. The insults and the blows mattered little, and I was happy to see Ross get out of the kitchen and go through the doorway that led to his bedroom.

Ross's bedroom had been transformed into a secret place away from her. Perhaps it was just in my mind that it was so, because I knew she had no idea of the fun my hero and I had in his room. It was here that we listened to his forty-five-rpm records of the Beatles on the Green Apple label. He had a turntable and speakers for them: the Beatles, Creedence Clearwater Revival, and the Doors were just a few. My hero seemed to cherish the Beatles' Green Apple label forty-fives more than his other records. So, of course, they were my favorite band, too.

Above his bed on one side of the wall was a large picture of a blue shark with its mouth opening to show the teeth and the powerful jaws of doom. It was especially cool to me—I always knew that it was nothing compared to her.

On the opposite wall was a poster of Farah Fawcett in her swimsuit. The poster was in no way pornographic, but for a kid my age, it was the sexiest thing I had ever seen. On the ceiling directly over the bed was a very colorful maze design of orange, green, blue, red, and yellow that started on the outermost portions of the poster and spun toward the middle, getting smaller and smaller as if to spiral into eternity. This was so different from the collection of old junk in my room; I spent as much time there with Ross as I was allowed.

The best part of summer included placing the record player strategically on the windowsill, just enough to operate it from the backyard and hear the music. This was a sure sign that the pool was open for summer.

Our backyard was divided into two main areas, the patio and the slope. The slope was past the patio and led into our neighbor's yard, which was about forty feet lower than ours. The view from the large bay window in our house was spectacular. I could see the lights on the towers of the Golden Gate Bridge flashing red in the fog, the ocean, and the streets at night as they led closer and closer to the city. Sometimes I could watch the fog roll in right before my eyes like the mist on some old scary movie as it crawls along the ground.

Keith and I had a strange little game we played called "tower's on." Whichever one of us saw the red lights turn on first, due to the heavy fog, would call out: "Tower's on"—and would be the winner. It's the funny kind of game a lot of brothers have with each other, I suppose.

The window at the back of our living room was the biggest I had ever seen in anyone's house. It must have been six feet tall and fifteen feet long, one solid piece of glass. What a view; it accounted for one of my few good memories in that house.

The patio portion of the backyard must have been one hundred twenty-five feet square and had a swirling design.

This is where the pool would be set up, just below the dining room windows. The pool took up the entire cement portion of the backyard. It was nearly five feet high and held what seemed to be a million gallons of water. When the setup was complete, we had the time of our lives outside the house. Josh and his younger brother, Kevin, were often in the pool with us. We felt alive while searching through the rubble of junk in the basement to find the old diving masks and snorkels. We used them as we pretended to dive for gold.

When Mom wasn't looking, Ross would toss coins to the pool below from the dining room window. My hero made it a point to make me feel safe in such deep water. I was old enough to stand and barely keep my head above water. He and his older friends would swim around the outermost part of the pool to cause a whirlpool effect. Around and around, until the motion of the water would carry even them. Petrified from the fear of drowning, I would reach for my hero's hand, knowing it would always be there, and he always was.

"I gotcha, buddy," he said.

We were always being too rough, too noisy, too messy, splashing too much water, or too something-or-other for my mother. It was never that we were just being kids. The record player would be playing some of Ross's records and the sun would be shining as the yard was filled with the laughter of the kids and the few neighbors who dared to enter the yard. Whenever it was obvious that we were having fun, Mom would be in torment because she wasn't in control. One punishment she created was for me to watch from the dining room window and see my brothers playing in the pool. I had to stand inside the house, dripping wet, and share her loneliness as the other kids played in the pool.

The fence between our house and the house next door was only three feet tall. Escaping into Betty's backyard was a sure way to get away from Mom, on the rare occasions that she would allow our relationship to be seen outdoors. Betty, the next-door neighbor, was an older woman who had lost her husband years before. An officer's wife, Mrs. Colonel James Townsend was always proper and well dressed. Very social and graceful, she always had the ability to catch me in her backyard. She never really minded; she just wanted to make sure I knew she was aware of my presence. Her backyard was a maze of steps and plants, well kept and all in perfect order. It was a great place to just get away, to walk around and think.

My hero would often hide in the backyards during games we would play. Finding him was no easy task. Perhaps he had made it so, just to have time away from me, but that was okay with me. My hero could do no wrong.

"Get the kids together, Richard. It's time for War," he said.

I knew immediately what that meant. I would scour the neighbors' yards for Josh and his brother, Kevin, just as Ross commanded. Once gathered together, the kids, all much taller than I, would be divided into two teams. I always made it onto Ross's team, never knowing why, just happy to be there. War meant the most serious of games. This wasn't for kids—it was for the big boys to play. My brother Keith was often excluded simply because of his age. Scott was always excluded out of pure sibling rivalry. My hero made sure of that.

At the bottom of Crestline Avenue stood the battle-ground known as Westmore Hill. The objective was to divide into two teams, one being the hunters and the other the guards. The game was commonly known as Capture the Flag. The battlefield was the entire hill itself; it must have covered thousands of yards of grass and more than that in cemented areas.

Sometimes, when the other kids couldn't be found or the games were getting too long to play, Ross and I would just spend time on the far side of Westmore Hill. Here we would slide down the hill on cardboard or even on the damp grass and our jeans. It was always the best when my oldest brother would try to slide farther than me.

I felt as if I had a companion and a mentor, someone who knew what I was going through and yet loved me and was happy to be around me.

As the summer days passed, the punishment sessions with Mom became more routine. Once I came in from playing, Mom would be waiting for me and yell and scream about something I'd done while I was outside. She had apparently been watching me and looking for any reason to beat me. It was as if I was a prisoner in a camp and she was the guard. Often Mom would hit me or kick me for excluding Scott from playing with me or tormenting Keith while I played. I began to believe that this truly was my purpose in life: I was created to be available for any rage that she needed to dissipate. I had been born into this family as a servant and a means of escape for Mom. As this idea took hold of me more and more, I struggled to find ways to change my destiny and become something bigger, something of value. My hero, Ross, would often reassure me that I wasn't supposed to be in this situation and to be patient. He said that things would change soon enough. I desperately wanted to believe him.

It became my duty to open the garage door at night whenever my hero came home from work. It was easier for him to blow the horn than to get out and walk the ten feet to the door and open it himself. Not minding, as I knew that I was in some small way repaying him for his kindnesses, I fulfilled my duty each time, often lying awake waiting for the horn to blow.

Summer also meant spending time washing and cleaning the old Dodge Polara ex–California Highway Patrol car he kept with great pride. It was just like the ones on the TV show *CHiPs*. We would wash it constantly, as it was unacceptable to have even the slightest amount of dirt anywhere. That big black car had more polish on it than most new cars out of the showroom. The large black push bars on the front were overpowering. Just the intimidating effect those push bars added would make him proud. He worked very hard to earn the money for the car and was proud to show it off. But never half as proud as I was. I felt that in some small way I was entitled to have pride in the car as well.

On weekends, shortly after washing the car, we would take it for a short spin somewhere. It could be anywhere, just to get away. Sometimes it would be down to Rolling Pin Donuts.

Rolling Pin Donuts was a place that only the big kids went to. The cars in the parking lot and the clothes and the attitudes of the older kids were all a sure sign that I was out of my league—or would've been, if it hadn't been for my hero.

I can't recall a single time that I was asked to leave or to give him space. He knew what I was going through and he was there for me, even if he wasn't open about it. He was there, and that is all that mattered. His knowing what was happening and being able to show support was good enough for me. He never made me feel like the small redheaded, freckle-faced kid brother.

As the summer went on and turned to fall, he spent more and more time away from the house and away from me. I knew that something was wrong, because he not only became distant but sought solitude of his own, too. He often went into San Francisco by means of the Bay Area Rapid Transit, never telling me what he was doing. I could tell that it was a serious matter. He had to keep quiet.

I had never been in the city without being in the back of the old gray station wagon as we went to Father's firehouse or someplace Mom needed to go. I could only imagine the things my hero was seeing and the feeling of freedom he must have enjoyed. Being able to do what you wanted, with a few bucks in your pocket, was still only a dream that I would fulfill one day.

I will always remember that day, the day I was told that he would be leaving for the army and was to finally start his life. He was proud of his accomplishment, but I was crushed. The look in his eyes told me he was not only happy, but also proud. I tried desperately not to show my disappointment. I knew he was leaving and would never return. I knew he was going to leave me behind.

Almost instantly I knew what the trips on BART were for. He had been taking tests and fulfilling the requirements to enter the military. Keeping this a secret was apparently required, since Mom's reaction might be devastating for those left behind, or perhaps even for him. He wanted out so badly that he would have done just about anything.

As I walked to school on the morning that he was to leave for Alabama and basic training, I looked down from the top of Westmore Hill and saw him being driven off in the recruiter's green Volare four-door. I knew what he had done.

He found an opportunity to get out of the house and he took it. As the car drove down the street and turned the corner toward the city, I found myself running parallel to it on the top of the hill, yelling, "Please don't! Please don't go, Ross!"

Somehow I expected him to stop the car and run out for a hug or a simple good-bye. But the car kept moving, and I couldn't help but feel that I had been deserted. First Dad and then David and now Ross—I was now truly alone.

No one to protect me. No one to understand what was happening to me. No one to help me get away from it all.

As I tried to understand that his desire to get out was more powerful than his desire to stay with me, I became angrier, even though I knew that if I had been presented with the same option, I would have gotten out, too, never looking back.

It is hard to communicate the conflict of these two emotions in my heart. On the one hand was the desperate desire to escape, and on the other was the guilt in leaving others behind.

As Mom realized that her oldest boy had left at the first chance he legally had, it changed her attitude. Deliberately, she re-created a family structure in her mind. Paying attention to every detail, she handed out special responsibilities to the ones left behind. Scott now became the father figure, often supporting Mom as she concocted her disciplines. She made sure that he was always on her side. She carefully plotted his moves, and as he became more and more supportive of her, they continued to be sort of friends.

Again, this was just another sword to stick in my side. Now it was more official. I was the one without value, worth, or any reason for being alive other than to be there when she needed to let it all out. She made that clear, informing me that I was lucky to be in her family and that I was an outsider trying to fit in. I was never addressed as her son anymore, only as "Nixon."

When President Richard Nixon was in office, Mom had despised the man. She'd made it clear that she thought he had no right to be where he was and that he couldn't be trusted. I suppose she felt the same way about me.

But I never let her know it gave me a sense of pride that she compared me to the president of the United States. Keeping this from her was one of the things that kept me going. No matter what she did or what stories she concocted, I had a value that she had actually given me. It was something that perhaps someday I could prove that I was worthy of—perhaps someday.

She now became possessive of the last untouched boy left in the home, the youngest, Keith. Maybe she was trying to make up for the two who got away. She tried to prove to herself that she was worthy of having children. Of course, I was a thing to be used by her at will, a thing to vent on, a worthless child, an emotionless cold child who refused to react.

With Dad gone, Ross in the service, and David in state custody, I was left behind to bear the wrath of Hell on my body, hidden from the world like some dirty secret. Mom had learned to change her approach. She had learned from David that she had to leave very little on the surface. As a child I wasn't aware of the changes she was making in herself or the changes in her family. All that was left was Scott, Keith, and me.

14

THERE'S LIFE OUT THERE

*I had tried so hard to stay out of trouble and keep a low pro-
file. Ross always told me to keep low whenever Mom was in
one of her moods. But Ross was gone now, and I didn't have
that extra set of eyes watching out for me. I was alone. It became so hard to find any sort of happiness. Most of my time
was spent thinking about Ross and what he was now doing.
I couldn't wait for the phone to ring so I could talk to Ross,
wherever he was.*

O VER TIME I came to terms with my current situation, and I came to believe that as long as I stayed as
insignificant as I could, it would make less trouble for me as I
went through life. Or so I thought.

Up the street near the corner of Crestline Avenue lived two
boys who loved sports. I didn't see them often other than to
play an occasional game of ball. Many of the kids in the
neighborhood liked sports, but these guys were crazy about
them. The house behind theirs had a couple of boys slightly
older than I. They were a small gang of kids, all friends with

one another. By now they were the only kids who were even close in age to me.

I had another friend who was a lot older than me named Ben. He lived just a few houses down the street. Ben was perhaps twenty-one and came from a completely different background. He lived with his sister and her husband. His parents were very nice and polite whenever they came by and I was there.

It became clear to me that since I didn't do well in sports, I had to find another way to fit in. So like most boys during the 1970s, I spent time hanging out thinking about girls, cars, and school. As we all became better friends, I was able to brush off the telltale marks of my beatings from Mom as passing rumbles with my brothers. They could all understand; they had older brothers themselves.

For the first time I found that all the things I thought about, other kids thought about, too. The wonderment of girls and the excitement of cars—I was shocked to learn that I wasn't the only one thinking about them. In some of the conversations we had, we shared the same questions and ideas about almost everything. I was happy to have other people to share and learn with.

Riding our bikes down Westmore Avenue past the bottom of the high school grounds and down Eastmore Avenue and the steep roads was always good for a break from the day-to-day routine. Terrace View Court hid an apartment complex, and I learned of this hidden jewel from my new paper route. The best place to ride bikes for miles was on the hills of Terrace View Court. We found a space just large enough to fit a bike between the barrier that separated the parking lot from the cliff and the hill below. The top of the heavily walked trail a few feet past the barrier was the beginning of an adventure that proved to be a learning experience for me. I can recall each time I started at the top of the long hill. The length and drop of the downward slope frightened me. It was nearly a hundred feet long and dropped some forty feet. Eventually it leveled off to a hilly trail with dirt paths going off in every direction. Wooden bike ramps of different heights were set up every thirty feet or so. Trails obviously worn by most of the kids in the neighborhood and years of overgrowth made this the perfect spot to test endurance and daring.

We found ourselves doing a variety of things in this forest that we would never do anywhere else, from making out with girls to smoking cigarettes in the woods and drinking beer. It was in these woods that I first learned how to smoke a joint. I never really got into marijuana. I found nothing exciting or interesting about it. But since some of the other kids did it, I had to as well. It was so important to be liked by the girls that I would have done almost anything. There were a few girls who said I was "cute" and liked to make out with me. There were a few others who thought I was weird, but didn't mind making out with me. Either way, I was being accepted for what I was. My self-image was okay—outside the house.

Although drinking was a popular pastime with the older kids, I never got into the spirit of it. I knew in my heart that drinking was half of Mom's problem. She was not only a drunk but also a nasty and cruel one. I just couldn't include it in my life.

We competed with each other to have the best bike parts or whatever the latest extras were. I learned what was required to be in the different cliques of "The Woods." I found being a paperboy helped out and kept me in step with the other kids.

Many envied my bike with the special Ashtabula rims and forks, the no-slip grips, and fat slick tires on the back. Before the end of that summer I had the most up-to-date and coolest bike around—and this bike wasn't leaving my side. Having had a bike stolen, I vowed to protect this one.

I discovered that I could share more and more with the other kids. I knew why they looked at me the way they did, and I was okay with that. The reason I looked as if I'd just gotten the crap beaten out of me was because I just had. They began to expect it after a while and simply brushed it off as "really weird parents."

I loved riding my bike to the top of Crestline Avenue, around the corner, then down Baldwin Avenue to the garage of my friends. There we could shoot the breeze and clean our bikes as if they were prized antique cars. I learned the most about people and girls there. I learned about sharing and what secrets really were, about what it means to be a friend and how to keep your mouth shut when you needed to. There were some things we always shared and some things we never dared to.

Two of the boys were more rebellious than I ever was, daring each other to perform violent deeds. They were interested in their fathers' collections of rifles and bullets in the garage. I felt uncomfortable being there once when they opened the cabinet and took out the rifles. They would brag and sound as if they knew how to load and fire them. I felt the fear and the butterflies in my stomach just like before.

They would make threats to use them against people they hated, people who were mean to them or kids in school.

"You want one of these to take care of your mother?" I was asked.

Shocked at the thought of anyone else thinking this, I carefully buried the idea and hid it away from the world. I had to assume that they weren't serious and wouldn't actually do it.

One such day I told them I had to go. I was just too uncomfortable with being around the rifles and the thoughts I had about my mother. The concept of actually going through with it was too much for me to deal with a second time. I may have held the thought a little longer than I should have, and yes, I was actually thinking about it, and yes, I would have done it. But I never did. As I rode back home I imagined what it would be like—what my life would be like if I was to go through with something as bad as that. I knew how I felt and wasn't going through that again.

Just after I made the turn at the top of Crestline Avenue, the most chilling sounds cut the air: gunshots, one after another. I stopped my bike and stood at the top of the street paralyzed by the fear that they had come from the garage I had just left. Not knowing what else to do, I simply froze as the silence afterward lingered. Not a bird was in the sky, not one sound could be heard. Total silence hung like a fog.

After a moment, I rode my bike down the hill and up to the basement door. I laid my bike down as I normally did and walked up to my room. Surprisingly, I made it to my room without being noticed. No one said a word as I sat on the top bunk looking out the window up the street, knowing that whatever had happened was bad.

At the same time, parents on both sides of the street came out into their front yards. Within a few minutes, police cars appeared at the top of the street and raced toward the bottom. As they reached the end, they parked their cars crosswise to prevent anyone from coming in or out. Two ambulances arrived at the bottom of the street and waited for entry, eventually being escorted to the top. The thoughts of that garage and of my friends being involved scared the life out of me. I knew it was their garage. I could feel that something had happened.

Finally I was told that two of the neighborhood kids had gone into their backyard with rifles, loaded them, and fired off three rounds. Apparently they were aiming for the massive tree in the center of the yard, but they missed.

Inexperienced with rifles as they were, they had no idea that the shots had screamed past the tree and into the bedroom of the neighbors behind them. Luckily, no one was hurt. But these neighbors had complained many times of the rowdiness of the kids who lived behind them, and now they had good reason to be upset.

Mom couldn't pass up the opportunity to find trouble in the neighborhood that didn't involve her and the police. She was out in the front yard with the rest of the parents in a flash once she heard the police cars. She immediately called my older brother and me out to the driveway. Seeing a police car racing down the street, she stepped off the curb, making it obvious that she wanted the car to stop. Once closer, the car stopped and the officer rolled down the window and forcefully told Mom, "Get those kids into the house—and get off the street!"

Ignoring the officer's instructions, Mom walked closer to the car and asked about what had happened.

"Several shots were fired into a house up the street—and we're looking for the shooter!"

Without losing a step Mom turned back toward us and yelled: "Get back in the garage—both of you."

As the garage door closed behind her she turned to Scott and said: "You go upstairs."

Looking at me, she said in a low, heavy voice: "You stay here!"

Right after the garage door had closed, she turned and glared at me as if she was completely sure I had something to do with this. I recognized the look on her face and ran toward the back of the garage.

The floor on the garage was smooth concrete that was always damp and often wet. Running past the left side of the car and looking back to see where she was, I slipped on the floor and slid into the side of the large wooden cart. My head hit the corner squarely and bounced off.

Stars filled my vision as I felt her grasp on my arm, pulling me up off the ground.

As the accusations flew out of her mouth, I could make out that she was sure I had shot someone and had run home to hide behind her protection.

"I'm not going to sit by and protect a piece of shit like you!" she screamed at me.

I was beginning to gather my thoughts as the stars began to fade and tried to let her know I had nothing to do with it. She pulled me in close to her face and said: "I don't care if you did or not. You're going to pay for it anyway!"

With all the force I could muster I screamed back at her: "I had nothing to do with it and you can't hurt me for something I didn't do!"

With that she grabbed the hair on the front of my head and shoved my head into the concrete. The back of my head hit the garage floor; the sound of bone hitting cement rings in my mind, even to this day. Heat rushed from the bottom of my spine to the top of my neck and filled my body. I felt no pain. I felt only the heat.

I braced for the worst. She continued to vent her anger: "You didn't go right to sleep last night!

"Your room is a pigsty!

"And now you're a killer!"

It became clear that this was just a chance to start another private session of her discipline. There was another slam of my head into the cement. Again I could hear that horrific sound.

My older brother came downstairs and asked: "What the hell have you done now?"

"IT's killed someone!" Mom screamed out.

That word—she said that word.

She called me IT.

She screamed at Scott: "He's the one who shot the people in the house up the street."

As my brother stood with a blank stare, she turned and dropped my head one last time. As the lights faded to dark I could hear her voice telling me to wipe the blood off my face and shirt and get upstairs to my room.

Lying on my back, I could hear nothing, feel nothing, and see nothing. I knew I was conscious, but I just lay there. After a few minutes I turned onto my side and looked at the concrete floor as my vision returned. With the return of my sight, the heat in my neck began to burn. The silence in my head became a screaming pain, as if I was being ripped apart. I could taste the metal fillings in my teeth and salt. Sitting up, I could tell that my hair was wet with blood. I fully expected more than what I noticed on my hands as I wiped the back of my neck. I crawled to the steps, up the first one and then the second one. I felt in my heart that she had done it this time.

I think I'm going to die, I thought.

I called to Scott knowing it was useless and fell face-first into the wooden step.

As silence settled around me, I realized that I was awake again. I could see my brother at the top of the steps, as he called out: "He's awake now."

Crushed with disappointment, I understood that he was just like Mom now. He had become part of her web. I recalled being her Little Nazi and how David must have felt once upon a time. I knew what she was doing to him and I understood.

As I looked up I could feel my face and hairline as it bled. I could see the red drops pooling on the hard wood step, and the sunshine that reflected off the floor. I looked at the blood and felt my shirt and face as she came downstairs. Swiftly she grabbed me by the arm and lifted me up off the step.

"Get up to your room. Now!"

I made it to my feet only to fall back down again. She grabbed my arm and shoved me forward toward the stairs. One step at a time, I focused on lifting each leg and holding my back up as I went. At the top I turned and fell to the side of the open doorway. Afraid I would fall back down, I reached for the door frame and hung on. She was right behind me, yelling: "Move! Move fast!"

Down the hall and in my room I could see the top bunk. Almost immediately the taste of salt and metal filled my mouth again and I fell to the floor.

Awake again, I found myself under the covers in my bed. She walked into the room and started yelling at me from the doorway.

"I'm going to turn you over to the police so fast it will make your head spin. I should have killed you when I had the chance. You worthless little piece of shit!"

Without moving a muscle I lay perfectly still, anticipating that as she got closer she would strike out and kill me. As she got nearer and nearer, her voice blasting out curses and anger, I placed my arms around my head just as she struck. I wasn't sure what she had in her hand, but it felt like a brick. Feeling the pain run from my ear to my jaw, from my wrist to my elbow, again I could see stars spinning in my head. My stomach tightened, and I was getting sick.

Since I was already in bed she had no need to check to see if I had become unconscious or had thrown up. As the stars faded away, smaller and smaller, her voice seemed to become fainter and fainter as she struck again. I recall the pain as she struck my chin and upper chest. Eventually I couldn't tell the difference between the darkness from the protection of the sheets and the darkness from her beating me.

Lying there, I became aware that she had gone and I was now alone. As I lifted my head from the covers and looked out the window at the foot of the bed, I could see that it was nearing dawn. Intending to see what damage she had done, I sat up and placed my feet over the bed. I wanted to jump down and go over to the mirror to take a look. As I sat up, I could feel the stars coming back. Thinking I was falling backward toward the bed, I allowed myself to fall, only to realize that I was falling forward and off the top bunk, onto the hardwood floor below. At the sound of my body crashing to the floor and my head bouncing off the hardwood she came rushing in, and laughed as she told me: "I thought you were old enough to stop falling out of bed, you stupid piece of shit."

I could tell as I looked up at her that she was well on her way to being loaded. It must have been six o'clock in the morning. Her speech and her posture were obvious, even to a boy. I was used to seeing her this way from time to time when something really bad happened to someone or when she went overboard while teaching IT his lesson of the day.

As I made my way to the bathroom, I attempted to pass her while she leaned against the doorway of my room. Confused and still half dazed, I tried to make it into the bathroom. Before I could turn on the light she reached in and pulled my arm.

"Back in bed!" she barked.

It was all she said as she went away.

As the sun broke through the darkness I gathered enough courage to try again. Carefully, I made it down the ladder to foot of the bed, where the old orange-and-white dresser once stood that held my ragged clothes. I grabbed whatever was on top of the pile in the underwear drawer from the closet and walked to the bathroom. As I passed the tall mirror in my room I could see that my hair was sticking up with dried blood. I reached the bathroom still dazed.

I have to get ready for school, I thought.

As I washed my face and hands, I could see the water change from clear to a purplish red. I stared at the water and realized that my life had been a circle of events that always came back to the beginning. Once again I started my day and wondered when would be the last time I would look at the water and see the blood.

It's come full circle—for a second time.

When I was nearly dressed she came back into my room. "What exactly are you doing?" she asked.

Confused, I stuttered my response: "I'm getting ready for school."

She simply looked down at me, and smiled. "Go ahead, get your butt out of here before you're late. Don't wait for Josh, just run, just run to school." She laughed.

Too exhausted to fight over it, I didn't bother to make sure the room was arranged and the furniture was in place as it all should have been each school morning. Then I remembered: *All that furniture is long gone.* I made my way down the hall, expecting some sort of response or acknowledgment that I was leaving the house as I passed the kitchen, where she sat drinking from that same old gray glass. It must have been 7:00 A.M. and nothing was said as I closed the door behind me and went down the pink concrete stairs.

The morning was clear, and a brisk dampness stuck to the silence as I walked past the bottom of Westmore Hill. There were no cars on the street, no sounds at all. I moved past the steps to the high school and toward the street that led down to school, and it hit me.

Where are all the cars?
Where are all the kids?

I began to realize that it had been summer vacation for nearly two weeks. I couldn't determine what day of the week it was or if it was summer or spring.

I walked past the swimming pool at the high school and down the side of the large building to the football field leading to the track field. A few people were running around the track exercising. None of them was a school student; they all appeared to be older.

I looked deep within myself and tried to piece my life together. Suddenly I recalled being younger, and how I'd treated David when he was still in the house. I thought about how I had made him feel. How I'd tormented him. How I'd watched when Mom beat him for things I did or lies I told about him. As they came faster and faster the recollections made me cry. I accepted the guilt as payment for being such a bad brother. I deserved whatever it was I got. I thought about how David was in the line of fire and how I had laughed at him. It was all becoming clear to me now. I had to make a decision.

I'm done—or one of us is going to die!

As I walk along back toward the pool I realized that my head was hanging down out of habit. Looking at the ground and being able to walk straight ahead was something I had mastered. It was time to change that, too—time to change my entire personality. It was time to become stronger and more outspoken; to express my thoughts and feelings, accepting nothing from anyone and giving nothing to everyone.

I will walk tall and without fear.

I will depend on no one.

"Most of all, I will not stand by and be hurt by anyone."

As I got closer and closer to Westmore Avenue my newfound confidence began to crumble. I began to worry that I was taking this way too far.

How am I going to do that?

How am I going to stand up to her?

Walking farther and passing the steps of the high school again, I looked over and saw the concrete for what it was, cold and hard, concrete that stood solidly, never moving and never giving in to anyone. I went up a few steps and made my way to the long open hall and the groups of trees that stood in the center of the high school courtyard. Then it hit me:

I don't have to fight back. I don't have to do anything.

All I have to do is blow the whistle. The school will step in and it'll be done. I'm about the same age as my brother when he was taken away.

As I started back toward home, it was decided.

It's over.

One way or another, it's over.

The walk from Westmore Hill to the house was no more than two hundred yards. Yet with each step I took closer to the house, I felt smaller and smaller. My spirit and determination were shrinking as I approached. All the previous feelings of strength and hope were melting away. I started to picture Mom in my mind; I could see her screaming in my face and hitting me for something. I felt like I did when I was a little kid. I so hated that instant and painful deflation of my hopes whenever I thought about Mom. As I walked up to the house it all came back to me, once again.

There's no way I can stand up to her.

I'm just too afraid.

15

DAD

I had trained myself to think about my words carefully before I spoke. Because of my stuttering and my fear of adults, I was focused on my thoughts and my words. The last thing I wanted was to say the wrong thing or give the wrong response. So it shocked me when I told my mother that my father was dead. Particularly since I found out about my father's death from that that same voice that had told me to "Stop and walk away" from Mom's bedside with the pistol in my hand. I was familiar with the voice, and yet it frightened me.

EARLY ONE MORNING, before our daily ritual of Mom chasing me around the house as punishment for whatever I was going to do wrong that day, I made my way to the kitchen. I found Mom at the table with her coffee and cigarettes.

Without warning, to either of us, I calmly announced, "Dad's dead."

I didn't know where the thought came from. I was shocked that I'd actually said it out loud. I had trained myself to hold back my thoughts from my tongue, and now I'd slipped.

Without hesitation Mom leapt out of the chair toward me and lashed out, slapping my face over and over as I tried to put my hands up to defend myself.

The eerie ringing of the phone suddenly silenced the sounds of her blows.

As if to prove me wrong, she slowly picked up the phone and without emotion listened without saying a word. She learned that her husband and father of her children, who had been in the hospital for a few weeks now, had died during the night.

Expressionless, she replaced the phone receiver, sat back down at the table, and lit another cigarette off the first as she stared out the window. My older brother Scott walked into the room and asked what the commotion was about.

The moment she realized that Scott was in the room, she knelt down and called for Keith.

Once Keith arrived in the kitchen she held both of them in her arms and coldly said: "Your father's dead!"

As I stood next to the refrigerator I watched her play on the emotions of the other boys. The entire time she spent holding them to her chest, she fired off cold stares right through me, to prove that she could exclude me from even the most emotional experience a family can go through. As she let them express their sorrow and pain, I started to become emotional. At the first sign of my tears she continued to hug the other boys and yelled to me: "Get in your room."

My first reaction was relief. I was spared from today's beating. In my room, I sat and wondered if Dad was in a better place now. I knew that even Hell was better.

He must be happy to get out, I thought.

Within a few hours the news had reached our relatives, who went through the motions and sent empty condolences. They must have known what had been going on in our house, and like everyone else they did nothing about it.

"Now that he and that other one are out of the way, we can carry on as a family," she said.

My father wasn't dead twenty-four hours when she and Scott decided to sell the house and move to Salt Lake City, Utah. Their talk of now being able to sell the house and use the proceeds of twenty-plus years of homeownership to cover the cost of the move made me ill. Mom and Scott talked about the great sums of money that they must be entitled to as a result of his death: the money from the house and his life insurance policies and the cash he had in his bank.

Of course, there were a few things that needed to be settled before the big move. Incidentals, like Dad's funeral and burial.

Right after Dad's death, Gram sent money and kept calling to see if Mom would acknowledge that she'd received it. Gram wanted to make sure that Mom looked presentable for the funeral. It was obvious that Gram was concerned about the way her daughter looked from the years of excessive drinking and smoking. Her daughter's self-destructive lifestyle had taken its toll on the once attractive and proud woman, who was now an embarrassment to herself, to her own mother, and to her own kids.

Gram sent enough money to allow Mom to get her hair done, get her nails done, and buy a nice outfit for the service. As the days passed, we received several calls from Gram wanting to know if she had bought the dress.

Mom was becoming more annoyed with each call. She needed a way out. As usual, she used the kids to support her lies.

After being coached for several hours and rehearsed until I was without error, I was instructed to call Gram and make it known how beautiful Mom looked with her new hairstyle and new dress for Dad's service. Though in reality she hadn't bought a thing other than another gallon of vodka for the day.

I was nervous when I placed the call. After only a few minutes, it became apparent that I was failing at the lie. Mom held the phone tightly between us, and she could hear me as I told the lies and recited details of the dress. Mom could hear Gram's replies, as she seemed to believe me. When I kept going on and on about the dress and her hair, though, it became clear that Mom was becoming angry. I described a different dress the second and third time I repeated myself to Gram on the phone. Without warning she exploded, twisting my arm to make sure I ended the call right then.

Once the phone was hung up she lashed out. One of the worst experiences I can recall was from that simple phone call I made to Salt Lake City. She turned around and shoved me into the stove. I felt the back of my head burn as I slammed against the black iron handle of the oven door. Before I even hit the floor she kicked me in the arm and chest. As I was fading in and out of consciousness I recalled David lying on the stovetop and Mom trying to turning on the burners and I became frightened. I tried to look up before I passed out and all I could see was Mom picking up the black cast-iron skillet she kept on the stove and glaring at me with those swollen red eyes. I tried to stand up, but I fell off balance and my head hit the black handle again. Before I could gather my senses Mom kneed me in the mouth while she held the iron pan in her hand. As the light started to fade to darkness, I knew that once again I was passing out. But the worst was yet to come.

When I awoke I found myself alone and in the kitchen. My face and eyes were swollen; I could barely see. My shoulder and arm were pounding with pain. Mom must have continued to kick and hit me as I was passed out on the floor. When I finally was able to sit up I felt the skillet on the floor next to me and turned to see the small drops of blood on the side of the handle. I knew why my arm and shoulder felt as if they were crushed. Mom must have taken a few swings with the iron pan as I lay unconscious on the floor. I was thankful that she hadn't hit me in the head with that pan.

Why didn't she?

What stopped her?

She could have killed me right there and it would have been over.

For nearly ten minutes I sat in the kitchen alone wondering what she had done to me as I'd lain on the floor. I felt the heat from my ears as I wiped away the dried blood.

It was just another day in the house of madness we lived in.

My father's funeral service was arranged at a church where I recalled being once before. The date was set and the family notified. To Mom, the members of the "family" would change depending on her mood. In her mind she controlled who was part of that elite and glorious organization. Most of the time Grandma and Mom's brother were excluded; I was always excluded. In her mind, I simply didn't exist now.

The service was short and meaningless as Mom played the part of the saddened widow. Right after the service we walked outside and were greeted again by hollow condolences. Mom was drunk—it was embarrassing.

Some of the faces I had seen before and recalled as family in distant memories; others I had never met. Standing off to the side was a thin, blond man in a uniform. I had no idea who he was as he stood waiting his turn to say his piece. When the small crowd finished, the man walked up and introduced himself as David, her son. IT.

Mom's mouth dropped and her face froze. Once she came back to her sense of reality, I could see the evil in her as it came to the surface, almost as if she was going to explode on him right there.

I don't recall the words that were exchanged in the short conversation between them. I know that Mom was demanding something from him. I really couldn't tell what it was or what significance it held to her. It was apparent that it meant a lot to her and that she had to retrieve it from David.

I do recall David getting slapped in the face, in front of God and everyone. As she frantically gathered her children around her and ordered us to the car, he walked away.

The curiosity was just too much for me and I had to ask: "Who was that?"

I'll never forget the look on her face. It was the most evil look I had seen on a person, ever. I was absolutely terrified. Frozen with panic, I assumed she was angry with me and was going to teach me a lesson right there. I didn't mind, due to our location. If God wasn't aware of the situation before, surely he would be now if she lashed out at me right in front his house.

She grabbed my arm and pulled me along to the car. I was sure I was going to get it.

"God, are you watching now?" I mumbled in hopeful prayer.

It was then that she told me it was David. She was furious over David's appearance at "her husband's funeral." He was never invited, according to Mom, and had no right to be there. "Who the hell does he think he is? Showing up to the boys' father's funeral in that uniform?"

That was the only time I ever saw David in uniform. It would be many more years before I would see his face again.

It's odd to say that I had no idea what kind of a man my father was. But I never really talked to him. I only recall seeing him on select occasions. And always when something occurred that would stick in my mind, these memories just happened to have Dad involved.

Most of the memories are of events such as Christmas or other family functions. At times it was as if we were *The Brady Bunch,* and other times *The Addams Family.* In either portrayal, the few memories I carry of Dad are clear and vibrant.

He was a fireman in San Francisco and was often out of the house working odd shifts or extra shifts. Most of the time he worked just to be out of the house, and who could blame him? I recall the hard black leather fireman's helmet he wore, the tall black boots, the silver-and-gold fireman's badge, and the smell of cigarette smoke combined with Old Spice.

Once, Dad came home to Crestline Avenue to say hello to the kids and to see Mom. His unshaved look, the smell of his cologne and cigarettes stuck in my mind. On the few occasions that I saw him, he often looked as if he had had a rough couple of days: evidence of the strain he must have been under.

This time Dad was standing just inside the doorway while talking to Mom and inquiring if he could take the kids out for a burger and catch up on things. Of course, we weren't allowed to go.

Dad stayed at the house a few hours and made a point of talking to each of the kids to see if things were better, or worse. I anxiously waited my turn, dancing around like a normal ten-year-old, as if I was impatient to sit on Santa's lap. I could tell by the tone of his voice and the genuine concern on his face that he knew exactly what was happening in the house. He knew which kids were at the receiving end of her anger and which were spared. It was as if he felt sorry for us; as if he could do nothing but just stand on the sidelines.

The times we went down to the firehouse to see Dad were always adventures. We used to walk up to the half doors and step over the entrance into the garage, where the fire trucks were kept. They were always clean and ready to go. The pride that emanated from the firehouse was obvious, even to a young boy.

The firehouse is where my father's extended family lived— Uncle This and Uncle That. I never could remember the names or the faces. All were men of the uniform who protected the city, each man the epitome of pride and dedication. The firehouse was always clean and organized. There wasn't a single toy on the floor—anywhere.

As it turned out, the trips to the firehouse were nothing more than to pick up Dad's paycheck. When I learned this, somehow, it changed the meaning of the visits. It wasn't just to let him see the boys or to catch up on things, or even to enjoy the faded hopes that Dad would actually step up this time.

Years afterward, I wondered just how Dad had survived when he turned his check over to Mom each payday. This went on for years, until the day he died.

How did he live? How could he? I always wondered.

His life at the firehouse made the facade work. The generosity of his comrades kept him alive. Their kindness and their complete disgust for his wife kept the other firemen close to Dad.

Eventually Dad must have become a drain on the other firemen and their families. It came to the point where his debts had to be paid in order to release his last check.

Apparently Dad had been on disability for a couple of years, and even then his checks went to her. With the miracle of direct deposit from state disability, there became no need to see him at the firehouse or wherever he was now living.

As a child, I would wonder just where he was or if he was even still alive. He had long since retired—as Mom put it—when he died. Perhaps a year had passed since the trips to the firehouse ended and the news came in that he was dead.

During that last year, I was told that Dad was living in a hotel.

The last memory I have of Dad is when most of the boys, all but David, were still in the house. The trips to see Dad at the hotel where he had been staying until he died were not for me. I wasn't allowed to see my father. Mom had told me, "You're an embarrassment. Why do you deserve to see him?"

She had made it very clear that only her family was allowed to see him, and I wasn't part of that. She had constantly reminded me, "If anyone finds out you are related to the boys there will be trouble."

To look at all of us side by side, it was apparent to most that I was different. I wore older clothes that were often dirty, and I usually held my head down unless spoken to or given a command. I didn't really care enough to notice that the other boys were talkative and appeared to enjoy life. Perhaps they did for a while.

Mom allowed the older boys to go see their father while I stayed home sick with curiosity. Once they returned I immediately inquired about every detail of what they'd seen.

"How is he? What's going to happen to him?" I asked.

All these questions would go unanswered. They themselves didn't know.

Ross told me in confidence that Dad was not at the hotel as I had been told, but rather at a hospital. It was apparent that he was dying. Ross tried his best to convince me it was for the best that I missed that part. Dad was a tall man and carried himself as larger than life, with a deep voice and hands that seemed to a child larger than anything. I cannot recall those hands striking out, ever.

Apparently Dad was now reduced to only a portion of the man in my memories. His weight, his looks, and his demeanor were now things of the past. He became a victim of lung cancer. Being a fireman may have been bad enough, but being a fireman who smoked made it worse. The separation from loved ones, the missing out on life's events must have hurt him deeply. For Dad, this was a sentence he had been serving for years now. Cigarettes were simply the vehicles of his destruction.

———————

Since I could only guess what was happening around me and wasn't allowed to be told, I asked Mom about Dad.

"Is he going to be all right? Can I please see him?"

All these and more questions were blown off as if they had little importance to her.

Just before he died, most of her time was spent talking to the San Francisco Fireman's Credit Union about the benefits she would receive as his "pending widow." I remember her being mean to people on the other end of the line to make sure they knew what she wanted. At the time, she was demanding the fullest of benefits for a man who wasn't even dead yet.

The week Dad died, Scott played the role of man of the house. He arranged for the Realtor to list the house and determine a time for the search in Salt Lake for the new one. At the time, I didn't understand why she would want to move to Salt Lake City, Utah. She had always said she hated her mother, who lived in Salt Lake. Now she wanted to live near her.

Mom reacted positively to the way Scott assumed so many responsibilities. She would often reassure him that he was growing up fast and successfully taking on the role of a real man.

Late at night I could hear them planning the trip to Salt Lake. They were careful to be sure that Uncle Dale, Gram's brother, wasn't involved. Mom was ashamed of herself and the way she raised her family in front of him.

I had told myself I was not going to be part of the move.

"I'm not going to Salt Lake. I'm not going anywhere. I'm done!" I said as I stared into the night. I felt a smile stretch across my face as I drifted off to sleep.

16

CALISTOGA

Unfortunately, I was not mentally or emotionally ready to stand up to her. Mom continued her warped campaign of abuse, which actually got worse after my father's death. But my world was yet again changing, and so was I. I had friends who were years older than I was. The freedom I experienced on a few occasions shaped my personality and gave me a foundation to build upon. I was changing, but I didn't know yet what or who I would become.

ONCE AGAIN the morning fog in Daly City is cold and wet. I realize that the sun has come up and the entire house is absolutely quiet. I lie in bed wondering what the day will bring. I get up, rushing to change into my sweats and high-top tennis shoes, make my bed, and get out of the house before she can get out of bed.

I arrive at Ben's house and knock on the window to his room. Once the window opens I can tell that he hasn't been asleep for long. As a fifteen-year-old, I'm curious what might keep a twenty-one-year-old single man up so late at night—

and so often, too. I have no idea just how narrow and small my world is. There are many things I don't know, but will soon learn about.

Within a few minutes the garage door opens and Ben appears ready to go jogging. We start out as we always do, walking down to the bottom of Westmore Hill and deciding which direction to go. Once we get started we talk about almost anything as we jog along. Often Ben inquires about new bruises or marks on my body. As always, I simply brush this off with some remark I assume he will accept and switch the conversation to him, asking what he's been up to or anything that isn't related to me. We always find comfort in each other's conversations.

Ben is the proud owner of a Honda 754 motorcycle. He allows me to help clean it or pass him tools for repairs when he works on it. Most of the time after the work is done and the bike needs a test drive, I ride on the back with him. I feel as if Ben's just like my brother Ross.

The freedom and excitement is worth the effort of cleaning the bike. If Mom ever finds out I'm riding a motorcycle, even as a passenger, I surely will pay the price. Still, I can't pass up the opportunity to be with someone who cares and enjoys my company.

On Saturday, when we arrive back home from jogging around Westmore Hill, we decide what to do for the morning, which usually involves doughnuts for breakfast. Rushing home to shower and change is the worst part of the morning, because I'm afraid that Mom will be awake and recharged for the day. Today I find the best clothes I can gather from the mountain of laundry kept on the full-sized pool table in my brothers' room and run back upstairs into the bathroom for a shower. As I'm about to close the door, not even looking behind me I can feel the fire running down the back of my head as she grabs a handful of my hair and pulls me backward to the floor.

"Just a reminder that I can catch you doing anything," she says.

I see the stare of her bloodshot eyes and smell that vodka morning breath. As my head drops to the floor she lets go. She shakes off the hair she's pulled from my head with her hand, and it falls in my face. I lie as still as I can. I know if I move or make a sound it might wake the demon inside her and cause the gates of hell to open yet again.

She walks away laughing out loud as she goes to the kitchen for her coffee and morning smoke. Once I stand up I close the door fast, but as quietly as possible. Running my fingers over the back of my head, I can tell she got a handful this time.

I'll take a shower and see what it looks like afterward, I think.

Since I'm running out of time, I rush in and out of the shower. One quick glance in the mirror and I see how obvious it is that something has happened to my hair; my scalp is still tender and red. Nonetheless, I get dressed and walk out the door down to Ben's house. The garage is open, and the bike is right where we left it. I wonder just how cool it would be to drive that huge motorcycle. Ben comes out of his room and asks if we're ready to go.

When he casually rubs my head as he walks by, I cringe and cry out. Horrified, he looks down at me; I have my head hung low from the embarrassment. He realizes what has happened again and apologizes, never discussing the cause, always just concerned with the effects. Ben is like another world for me, another place to be other than home.

He suggests that it's a better idea to take the car and not the bike this time as he puts the helmets back on the seat of the bike. I'm disappointed, but happy that we're doing something together.

Down past Westmore High School off Eastmore Avenue is Rolling Pin Donuts, the jewel I learned about from my brother Ross, who often bragged about the mint and lemon tea and the girls who worked there.

As always, the time flies away, and soon it is time to return to that place where I sleep, that special place called "Home."

There is quite a commotion and buzz around the house as I manage to blend into the background, but I can tell that Mom is excited about something. She is on the phone with Gram and seems happy. But this time it is almost genuine. I warn Gram, in my mind, that this is some kind of plot Mom is conjuring up to get something from her.

She hangs up and runs by me downstairs. Passing me as if I'm invisible, not even the simplest acknowledgment—which I guess is better than the alternative.

I follow her downstairs and listen just outside the door. I'm shocked to learn that we are really moving.

Mom has it all planned. She tells Scott, "We'll drive out to Salt Lake and find a house. Then we'll spend time at the Salt Flats. Keith will love it. We'll drive out to Utah and have a family vacation."

As the news registers in my mind I become excited. On the rare occasions that we're allowed to see Gram, she lets me play in her pool and with her golf clubs on the lawn. All the memories come flashing back in my mind and the happiness consumes me. I open the door and walk into the room excitedly. Mom simply turns, stops for a moment and stares at me, then returns to talking to my brother.

I am amazed at the plans and ideas flying out of her mouth. We are going on a vacation that has been long overdue, a family activity that will bond us together. It's too good to be true.

As always, this really *is* too good to be true. It has become very apparent that I'm caught up in the excitement. Mom stares at me and says, "The trip to Salt Lake is for my boys. You'll be staying behind to watch the house while we're gone. My boys need time to heal after the shock of their father's death."

I stand paralyzed by the news and angry at myself for getting caught up in the joy.

I should have known better, I think. *How could I allow myself, again, to get excited or show any positive emotion, knowing what the past has taught me?*

As I turn and walk out of the room I can still hear them talking, clearly enjoying the idea of a family trip. Up the stairs to my room I go. Turning the corner, I finally understand.

She will be in Salt Lake and I will be here alone.

This is perfect!

I can sleep at night and not worry about her.

I can eat all the food I want.

I can wash and wear clean clothes.

Just as I started to get excited, she comes into my room. "You will not be joining my family in Salt Lake. This is for family only."

I ask: "How long will you be gone?"

"A couple of weeks," she barks back at me. "We'll be on vacation. Then we'll be back for our things."

To ensure my safety, I put on the saddest face I can to make her believe that her twisted remarks, once again, have devastated me. But inside, I am ecstatic. She sees my sadness as genuine and walks out.

It worked!

"Go ahead. Go to Salt Lake! Go to China! Go to hell for all I care!"

All the possibilities fill my head. I have to let Ben know the great news. I look around and find her back on the phone to Salt Lake, this time to Aunt Amy and Uncle Tod. I slip out the front door and run down the street to find that Ben's car is gone. Turning around, I slowly walk back to the house. Then I see his green Mercury Cougar coming down the street. He waves and honks as I turn and follow the car back to his house.

"I've got the best news!" I quickly blurt out. "Mom and my brothers are going to Salt Lake City, Utah. I get to stay here and hang out!"

The excitement that I am expecting from him never appears. He looks dumbfounded.

"They're moving to Salt Lake City!" I exclaim with excitement.

Again, all he does is stare. As we walk back to the garage, Ben puts his arm around my neck and shakes my head. "What do you mean, moving?" he asks.

"Mom and Scott called Century Twenty-one. I heard her on the phone. She's going to sell the house and move away."

Ben walks over to the side of the garage, near the toolbox, and asks me to sit down. "What are you talking about?"

"Mom and my other brothers are moving to Salt Lake and I don't have to live with her anymore. Don't you get it? She's leaving!" I say.

"No, Richard—you don't get it!" he states. "She can't just leave a kid alone. She can't just move and leave you!" He is clearly angry. "Where are you going to stay? How will you eat? What will you use for money?" He fires off these questions at me as if he is mad at me.

As he keeps on talking I fade out and realize that he is right.
I have no money.
I have nothing.
I'm fifteen years old.
Once he realizes I have tuned him out, he stops and reassures me that it will all work out. After an odd and uncomfortable silence, he changes the subject and inquires if I can stay to help change the chain on the motorcycle. I happily stay and help.

The next Friday a Realtor from Century 21 came out and listed the house. By Monday morning the house was sold and we had fifteen days to leave. Mom had entered into an agreement to rent back the house for the fifteen days while she looked for a new one in Salt Lake.

By Wednesday the buyers closed on the house and Mom had a check in her hands. First thing Thursday morning she went down to the Chevrolet dealership to purchase a new car for the drive to Utah. It was the first time I had ever been to a car dealership. I spent most of my time marveling over the new cars, paying particular attention to the new Corvette. Sitting in the driver's seat, I felt as if I could take off and never look back.

Without warning, I felt the grasp of her hands on the back of my neck pulling me out of the car and onto the concrete floor. A swift kick to the ribs made sure I got the message: I was not to touch the car. She leaned down and whispered in my ear: "If you touch that car again, you'll pay dearly for it."

I gathered myself together and walked over to the windows. I could see Toys "R" Us across the street and recalled when times were better. Mom would take the boys, all of us, into the store and we could pick out any toy we wanted.

On the advice of Scott, Mom purchased a brand-new 1980 Chevrolet Citation. It was ridiculous—one of the most hideous cars I had ever seen. Paying cash for a car that barely fit four people was absolutely funny.

Driving the car home that night was an event. The neighbors came out to see what she had bought. All were interested in finding out how soon she was moving. Several people asked, "When?"

The only person who asked where was Susan, Josh's mom. His father, Fred, had a good idea of what was happening in my house, although he successfully held back his disgust. It was that week that I learned just what he thought of Mom and the boys.

As my brother finished packing the car I sat in my room waiting for the moment they were gone. For the first time in a long time I sat near the front room without fear. The anticipation was just too much. Shortly before they pulled out of the driveway, Mom came into my room to make sure I understood that the house must be kept just as she was leaving it. There were to be no problems of any sort. The new house for *her* family depended on it. She gave me sixty dollars and turned away.

As I watched from the bedroom window, they pulled out and down the street.

"Finally they're gone!" I exhale.

I waited all of ten minutes to get my coat and walk to Cala's Market. I bought all the food I wanted. The long walk back wasn't bad, as I anticipated having pizza, macaroni and cheese, and all the soda and chips I could eat. Just before dark, I arrived back at the house with my treasures.

As I unpacked the bags onto the kitchen table, the phone rang. It was Susan, across the street, inviting me over for dinner. I informed her that I'd just came back from the store and had already eaten my dinner.

"But thanks anyway," I told her.

Within moments Josh came over to confirm that Mom was gone and that I had the house to myself. He restated a few times that his dad couldn't believe she'd left me there alone. I told him how great it was, but I realized that his father was angry over it.

His father intimidated me. Anytime I called on Josh to play when Fred was home after work, I walked softly around him. Soon after Josh went back to the house, I got another call from Susan asking me to come over.

As I walked up the steps to his house I thought: *I'll just eat dinner and make my way back home afterward.* I didn't want to fuel any anger from Fred for staying at the house while Mom was off in Salt Lake.

Susan and Fred made it very clear that they felt it was wrong to leave me alone at home, and that they were available for anything I needed. I was shocked to realize that they were angry with Mom, not me. As I tried to explain that everything was more than okay with me, Fred forcefully reiterated that he understood I was happy with her being away, but he wasn't. I realized what Fred was really saying: He knew what was happening in the house and was glad to see me away from her.

Eventually I returned home to the living room and the TV. I had all the food I wanted. There would be no chores and no running away from her. I was in heaven. I stripped off my filthy clothes and lay around in my underwear watching TV. I slept on the sofa, and never even wanted to go to my own bed.

Early the next morning Ben called to check on me. It was nice knowing that people understood the situation and were concerned about me. It was a shame that I realized how many other people cared only days before the move.

Ben made it a point to let me pick something cool to do before the move. After we talked, I decided to take a motorcycle ride up to Calistoga, California. I had never been there. I had never been anywhere, really, and I was curious to see anything. I decided to go with Ben on the ride instead of staying at home with my best friend, Josh. It wasn't that I didn't want to be with my best friend; I did. But I couldn't pass up the chance to go somewhere I had never been before. I had only heard about the water parks, pools, all the food and the fun to be had. Plus, it was the chance to ride on the bike. It was all just too wonderful to miss.

I went off to JCPenney for a swimsuit. I calculated the cost of the food and how much money Mom had given me and decided there was enough for a swimsuit.

Once inside the store I realized that the swimsuits cost much less than I'd expected. Walking around the boys' clothes, I marveled at what the store had for sale. Everything was there on display. All the coats, pants, shirts, and even socks were brand-new. Not that I had never been in a store before, but being alone in one without being afraid to lift my eyes was a new experience. Before, it had been my duty to always look down and not comment on anything. This time I was walking free and took my time.

While walking around the store and observing others around me, I realized that I was different. There were other kids and their parents, walking, talking, and looking at me as they went by. I realized that I was filthy and my clothes were ragged. I must have looked like hell. I resolved to fix that right then and there. I was going to buy new clothes no matter what!

As I walked around the store I decided that a shirt, pants, and socks would be fine. I could get rid of them before Mom came back and before she even knew about it. I picked out a red shirt and blue corduroy pants and looked for white socks. Eventually I found my way to the right area and was almost in a stupor over the selection of not only socks, but underwear and T-shirts as well. Stunned at the whiteness of the packaged briefs, I thought about the ones I had on. My few pairs were unfit for car rags. I'd never given a thought to getting new ones until then. I knew I didn't have enough money for shirt, pants, socks, *and* underwear. Still, there I stood motionless in front of rows and rows of new clothes.

Finally I put back the pants, socks, and shirt and picked out several pairs of briefs, all different colors and fabric, all new, and all just for me. What a difference it would make if I could have something new that she couldn't see. Since I did my own laundry, she seldom even knew what clothes I had anyway. The thought of not being able to afford all that I needed was a dilemma, though. If I purchased the pants and shirts, then I couldn't afford the underwear and vice versa. I decided that I had to have both.

Carefully I selected several pairs of briefs and then made my way back to the pants and shirts. I tucked the packages of underwear into the legs of the pants and walked over to the dressing area. Once inside the dressing area I opened the packages of briefs and put them on, one after another. I put on three or four pairs and then proceeded to put on my old pants. I stuffed the empty packages into my pockets and walked out. I was sure that I looked funny and would get caught. After leaving the dressing room, I simply put the pants and shirts that I'd selected on the counter and paid the bill for them. Quickly turning around, I left the store and never looked back.

I knew that stealing was wrong, but I just couldn't pass up the chance to get rid of the same pants and shirt I had been wearing every single day for more than a year.

On the bus back to Crestline Avenue, I realized that I'd forgotten to get what I'd gone there for in the first place: a swimsuit. As I walked down the street I saw Ben in the front of his house cleaning the car. I quickly ran up to my house and into the bedroom. I stripped down and placed the stolen underwear in the bottom of a drawer. Quickly getting dressed again, I returned to the garage and out onto the street. Ben flagged me down and asked what I was up to with my new freedom. Jokingly, I replied that I had purchased a swimsuit for the trip.

"That's great! Let's see it."

Unable to produce one to show him, I was embarrassed, as it became apparent that I had lied. I hung my head down low and said: "I bought something else. I got them because I really needed them. I don't have any clean ones and—"

Ben interrupted to say: "What are you talking about, Richard?"

I dropped my head lower and softly whispered, "Underwear."

Ben asked me: "Why did you say a swimsuit? Were you embarrassed to say underwear?"

"No!" I replied. Even though I was. "I just didn't want to let anyone know I needed them."

Not realizing the desperation of my situation, Ben asked about my clothes and what I owned. As I told him about my one pair of summer pants and one shirt, and the winter pants and winter shirt I was "going" to get, he just stood there for a moment—no reaction at all.

"Okay, I've had enough," he said. "We're going to Sears."

That day Ben bought me everything he knew I needed, including the swimming trunks. Ben had often talked about Mom and how he thought she was mentally ill. He'd never accused her of being bad, just sick.

I now realized that others saw her for what she was. I wasn't the only one. The boys down the street, Josh's father and mother, Tony and Alice next door—they all commented that week on her and the way she treated me.

That night I showered and simply lay around the house in my new yellow-and-blue briefs, watching the lights from the San Francisco Bay Bridge and the red flashes on top of the power lines across the bay. As I fell asleep to absolute quiet and complete lack of fear, I realized that there was more to life than what I was living.

When the phone rang the next morning, I became aware that I had slept through the night, a major accomplishment for someone who fears the dark and the evil sounds so common in that house. Sounds like the door opening in the middle of the night, knowing it was her as she lashed out at me just for being asleep. I was always supposed to stay awake until she came in to tell me good night and recap all the things I'd done wrong that day. Even if she never came in, I was to await her arrival.

On the phone, Josh asked if I wanted to come over for breakfast. Unsure what time it was, I rushed to clean up and made it across the street in record time. Very proud of the fact that I was clean and had new clean clothes, I felt comfortable. For the first time I walked past Josh's father and felt confident. As we sat around the table, Susan made breakfast burritos and poured milk for all. It was wonderful to have hot food and as much of it as I wanted.

The kids—Josh, Kevin, and Donna—were all in a hurry to leave the table and go about their business, all talking to each other as freely as they wanted. It was more commotion than I had seen in a long time. Once Josh realized that I was in no hurry, he left and his father stayed with me at the table as I ate what seemed to be four times my share.

He never said a word to me about my manners, my clothes, or anything. I was made to feel welcome. I wondered if perhaps Fred was somehow giving me his approval for taking control of the situation and making the best of it. It was the first time I can recall being in his house unembarrassed about the way I looked. So many times before, I would walk as fast as I could past his recliner and down the stairs to Josh and Kevin's room. Often I could hear him comment under his breath about the way I looked and how much of a shame it was that Mom got away with it.

As soon as I returned home from breakfast, I quickly packed my new clothes and went down to Ben's house. We were to leave that morning. The anticipation was just too much. I imagined the places we would see and the freedom we would feel on the bike as we cut through the wind down the most beautiful roads in California.

I handed Ben my bag and he secured it to the back of the bike. Obviously excited, he reminded me: "You need to be careful and lean with me in the curves. Hold on tight."

Almost drooling with anticipation, I listened to every word.

As we rode out of the city, I realized I had underestimated the beauty of California. The trees with all their colors, the miles of endless blacktop roads, and the smell of the air were almost spiritual. I recorded the scenes in my mind as they passed by. California was like a dream to me.

Near Calistoga we found a little snack place that fit right into the surroundings and scenery. We sat and talked about old times, when I'd helped him with his bike or the car, or we'd jogged around Westmore Hill. In an odd sort of way, recalling these memories was almost sad.

Once our snack was over, we returned to the road and our destination. Shortly afterward, Calistoga came into view. The signs on the side of the road and the billboards became more frequent as we rode through the town. Turning off the main road, we found our destination.

Within a moment we turned into the water park and parked the bike. As we walked to the entrance I inquired if he knew how much the admission was.

"Don't worry," he said. "I got you covered."

I felt a sense of brotherly love. We spent the day in and out of every water ride you could imagine, chasing each other from line to line. We wore ourselves out and enjoyed every minute of it. Before we knew it the sun started to set; the day was coming to a close.

Content with the time we had together, we returned to the motorcycle and realized the ride back wouldn't be as much fun as the trip up. With both of us tired, it would be a long ride. As he drove, Ben reminded me a few times that I needed to lean into the curves with him. Completely exhausted, I tried my best to do as he said. Soon we were home. As we stepped off the bike, the air was dark and cold. The dampness of fog combined with the dampness of my new jeans added to my exhaustion.

I knew the walk back to the house would be tiring. When Ben asked if I wanted to sleep on the couch in his room, without hesitation I told him: "Yes!"

Once inside, we simply dropped our bags on the floor and walked into the house. He showed me the couch in his room and asked me to wait there until he found a sheet and blanket. I grabbed my bag, reached for a dry pair of briefs and socks, and changed. As I sat on the side of his bed I could feel my eyes closing. Unintentionally, I fell into the bed and was asleep before I hit the mattress.

Returning to the room, he simply covered me with a blanket and tucked a pillow under my head. It was the most restful and peaceful sleep I could recall. Completely comfortable and unafraid, I slept soundly with my eyes closed.

17

WELCOME BACK

*After Dad's death, I took to heart the fact that so many peo-
ple had disappeared from my life. Dad, David, and Ross
were each on their own journeys and had left me behind. I
was nearly sixteen years old when I found something within
myself that scared me—a feeling that erupted to the surface
like a volcano. Anger. I had thought I was able to show Mom
that I wasn't about to be treated like some circus freak anymore. But when I tried to stand up for myself, that little
red-haired, freckle-faced boy was inside my teenage body. I
was still a timid little boy and I hated myself for it.*

THE NEXT FEW DAYS were spent simply enjoying
the peace and quiet that filled the house. I could stay
up as late as I wanted or sleep soundly without reservations
or fear. In the back of my mind I knew that she would be
home eventually. As the days passed and the scheduled date
for Mom's return came closer, the anxiety took away from my
incredible joy at being alone.

Between eating dinner at Josh's house and spending time with Ben, the days flew. Before long the two weeks were up and "D-Day" was approaching. That Friday morning when Mom and my brothers were to return to the house, I woke and went from room to room to clean up any mess I had left. Everything had to be just right. By lunchtime I had completed my chores and went down the street looking for Ben. I thought one last afternoon of fun would be a good idea.

As I walked down the street I could see that his car was gone. I turned around and looked at Josh's house to see if there was any sign that he was home. No such luck. It didn't really matter that much to me as I walked back up the street to the house. Once inside, I thought of all the questions that Mom would ask me when she got me in the basement alone:

How much money did you spend and on what?

What did you do for two weeks while I was gone?

Who did you have over?

On and on I went through the list in my head and tried to find answers that would satisfy her. I knew that nothing would satisfy her if she was in one of her moods.

Since it was only shortly after noon, I decided to take the bus from the top of the street down to Westgate Shopping Center and walk around. I had nearly twenty-five dollars left and thought I should spend it now. The bus ride was only about twenty minutes straight down Southgate Avenue. At the mall I went directly to Adeline Bakery, one of Daly City's best bakeries. They always had the freshest doughnuts and pastries anywhere. I selected a few and walked the mall with my bag of treats. Window-shopping was sort of new to me, as I had never really been allowed to with Mom.

From store to store, I walked and stopped at the signs and displays in the windows. Near the end of the mall was King Norman's toy store. Once inside, I went right to the remote-control cars and boats. I'd always wanted one to play with. Scott had several Cox gas-powered airplanes he tried to fly around the street and down at Westmore Hill. I could only imagine the fun he must have had. From the toy store I walked around to the department store near the front of the mall.

The large display of new clothes for kids and teens tempted me. JCPenney had massive windows with several displays. As I walked around to the front, I decided to look at the blue jeans to see how much they were. I knew that Mom would never notice if I bought clothes and forgot to tell her. Into the store and through the various departments I walked, marveling again at all the clothes.

In the young men's department there was a display of Boy Scout and Cub Scout uniforms. I saw a large counter with what must have been a hundred different patches and badges for sale. I walked around and recalled the uniforms that my older brothers wore when they'd been scouts. I recalled the yellow-and-blue scarf tied around David's neck that held a gold scout clip and the blue-and-yellow-striped cap he wore.

When I was younger, I never understood why he was allowed in Cub Scouts or why Mom stopped being a den mother. I always hoped that someday I could have the opportunity to be part of a group like that. Unfortunately, that day never came. I had faint memories of Dad standing next to my oldest brother in his Cub Scout uniform. It was another one of the few memories I had of Dad in the house.

Before long, I found the clothes I wanted to buy and had just enough money for, and this time I was going to pay for them.

I missed the scheduled bus that would leave me just enough time before Mom was supposed to be back. Anxious for the next bus, I waited and waited. I knew I had to get home and put the clothes in my dresser in the closet. Eventually I made it to the top of Crestline Avenue, where the bus dropped me off and I ran down the street home. As I passed one house after another I could see my house getting closer and closer. I couldn't see a car in the driveway or on the street, so either she'd parked in the garage or I had made it home before she did. Running into the front yard, I could see that the garage door was closed. I made it to the front of the house and looked into the windows of the garage and found it empty. I had made it home before she did.

I walked up the steps to the front door winded and tired. Once inside, I went to the kitchen for a glass of juice and to sit for a minute. I opened all the packages and placed the empty packs in the kitchen trash. I opened the dresser in the closet and realized that I had a few pairs of new colored underwear from the week before. I was afraid that perhaps I had gone overboard and now had too many. The bottom drawer was nearly empty and seldom used. I folded and placed the new briefs in the drawer and went back to the kitchen.

I took one last walk through the house to make sure that everything was in place for her return. As I walked past the kitchen and into the hallway, I could see the trash can, with the empty underwear package from JCPenney on top. If Mom ever saw that, she would know what I'd bought and flip out. I grabbed a new liner and took the trash bag into the basement and put it into the trash cans near the garage door.

Back upstairs and onto the couch I went. Exhausted from running around and all the stress of the day, I lay there looking out the big bay window at San Francisco. In what seemed like a few minutes I had apparently fallen asleep.

I awoke to the sound of the garage door opening and the car pulling inside. It was near dusk and much later than Mom had said she would be home. By the time I gathered my thoughts together, Scott came up into the front room and sat down in a chair opposite the couch.

"What have you been doing while I was away?" was all he said.

He made it sound like I was to report to him on all my activities for the past two weeks. Angered by his sense of authority I simply replied: "Piss off!" as I walked back to my room.

Like a flash, my older brother ran to the top of the stairs where Mom had just arrived.

"Richard swore at me and says he hates all of us," he said.

As I heard the story being laid out for Mom to stew over, I knew that I had fallen right into his little trap once again. Surprisingly enough, Mom didn't seem to care. She walked right past him down the hallway as I watched. After she made it to the kitchen, I could hear the cabinet open and the sound of her glass and the bottle clanking against each other as she poured the first of many shots for the evening.

Before long my younger brother walked in the room and sat down on the lower bunk bed. Without hesitating he told me about the new house and the neighborhood. He had selected a room on the top floor next to Mom's room, and my older brother had selected a room downstairs.

"Mom picked the biggest room for Ross and made sure that no one else can have it," he told me, mimicking the way Mom slurred.

"He's in the army and never coming home. Why does he need a room, and why the biggest?" I asked, knowing the answer already.

When Ross left the house Mom informed all of us that he was simply gone for training and would be back home at a base near San Francisco. She convinced herself that he was not running away but temporarily sowing his wild oats. Nothing could have been farther from the truth. He was gone and gone for good. No one would blame him if he never set foot in California again. Anxiously, I asked Keith the big question: "Do I have a room?"

"Yes, it's downstairs between Scott's room and the laundry room. It's not very big, but since you weren't there to pick one, you got what was left over," he said.

"Since I wasn't there? What about Ross—he wasn't there, and he's never going to be there!" I yelled back at him. "How come he got the biggest room?"

Hearing the volume of my voice, Mom came into the room and told Keith to go down and unload the car. Once he was out of sight she leaned over and told me: "I'm not sure you're coming to Salt Lake with my family. So you'd better watch your step around me or I'll leave your ass alone on the curbside."

Instantly I returned to the fear that she was so good at instilling in me. She turned and walked away into the kitchen for a few more rounds with the vodka.

After a quiet and uneventful dinner I cleaned the dishes as usual and went to bed. I could hear the other boys and Mom talking about the new house and all the things they needed to get done before the move, and talk about cleaning out the basement and yard. Mom and Scott were making decisions like husband and wife—in Mom's eyes, Scott had taken Dad's place.

Sometime after the other boys had gone to sleep and Mom had enough time to put herself nearly into a liquid coma, she came in my room and ordered me to get out of bed. She was careful to not speak too loudly, because my younger brother was asleep in the bunk beneath me. Once I was down from the bed she grabbed my ear and pulled me out of the room.

"Don't you dare wake Keith up or I'll kill you," she whispered to me.

I was about to cry out from the pain of her pulling my ear when I looked into her eyes and realized that she was absolutely loaded.

In the kitchen she stood near the table, took a shot of vodka, and stared at me as she swallowed. Then she slowly walked over to the dining room table in the next room; I could see all kinds of trash scattered on the table. She had taken the trash out of the garbage cans downstairs and sifted through it to see what I had thrown away during the week.

"What the hell is this?" She was holding up an empty Styrofoam container from one of my lunches with Ben.

"It's from Denny's when . . ." was all I could get out before she pulled out a smaller bag of empty soda cans.

"What about these?"

"They're soda cans," I replied, confused at what the issue was.

"Those were for the boys, not you. Just who the hell do you think you are, anyway? I bought them for the boys, not you. You stupid stuttering ass!" she yelled.

As she kept yelling, my heart sank. I knew she was going to find the empty packages of underwear I had bought and would flip. Before I finished the thought in my head she pulled out several empty packages. "And what the *fuck* is this? Do you mean to tell me you bought clothes without my permission?" she screamed.

"I needed them and had more than enough money," I said.

"That was my fault for leaving you with any money at all," she barked back. "You should have eaten out of the trash, for all I care."

With fire in her eyes she walked back into the kitchen, grabbed my shirt under the collar, and pulled my face close to hers. The smell of the vodka overpowered me.

"You go in that room and get all the underwear you bought and bring it here right now," she commanded.

As she let go of my shirt I could feel the anger growing inside me. That sense of sheer anger, the kind that got me in trouble the last time I'd mouthed off to her. It was like a volcano. I could feel the adrenaline running through my chest. I was sure I was going to explode. As I looked in her eyes, I found a glimpse of courage in myself.

Don't do it, Richard.

Don't let it go.

Just hold on.

I wasn't the shy little redhead from years before. I was now fifteen and nearly six feet tall. Yet somehow she had the ability to make me feel like I was that helpless child once again.

Something inside me told me to back down and let her have her way; she was far too drunk to mess with, not today. I pulled open the middle drawer and found the clothes that I had bought when Ben and I went to Calistoga. I recalled the fun we had as I held the swim trunks and the clothes that he had bought for me.

"Don't you keep me waiting, boy," she called out.

The sound of her voice—and more so, the tone of her cackle—reopened the gates within my heart. Anger was bubbling inside me. I was close to exploding. However, I quietly backed down and closed my eyes as I focused on what she said to me.

I knew that when she referred to me as "boy," she was close to losing it. I quickly put down the swim trunks and gathered the colored briefs that Ben had bought for me. I knew that the ones I had stolen were in the middle drawer, safe from her.

"Get your ass in the kitchen, *now!*"

Slowly I walked back to the kitchen, expecting the worst. She followed two steps behind me, quiet until we made it into the kitchen. Without warning she shoved me forward and forced me to the floor, kicking me and yelling at me that I had again broken her trust.

"You just don't get it do you? I know everything you do. Everything! There is nothing you can do without me knowing."

The entire time she was yelling, she kicked and kicked. Moving away from her reach, I crawled toward the dining room table as she backed down and let me stand up.

The fire from within me now started to burn and I could tell that I was going to erupt.

Don't lose it now.

Just hold on!

Just hold on! I kept saying to myself, over and over in my head.

As she continued to yell at me for everything I had ever done wrong in my life, I faded out of listening and started my daydream of what I wanted to do to her.

I picture myself—slowly turning around and walking directly up to her face. I see the look in her eyes change from anger to fear in a moment when I say to her: *It's over! Never again will you . . .*

As I tell her that she will never kick me again, I step back and kick her to the floor. I tell her she will never beat me unconscious again as I deliver kick after kick. I kick her chest, her head, and her stomach. For a moment, I see myself on the floor next to the refrigerator—lying unconscious. I tell her: "And you'll never choke me unconscious again" as I place my foot across her throat and step hard enough to stop her breathing—just as she did to me.

I see myself kneeling down and lifting the back of her head, grabbing hold of her hair as I slam her head into the floor over and over.

———————

In my daydream—I was actually fighting back.

I was brought back to reality and the situation at hand as I heard her scream: "Now—take all of those briefs and throw them on top of the garbage!"

The entire table had been covered with the trash she had dumped. Garbage was spilling onto the floor around the table. With an air of uncertainty I obeyed. I was tossing them up on the pile and looked back at her.

"Turn around. Don't you look at me!" she commanded.

Again the smell of booze filled the air. With a careless attitude, I turned my head and body around to face the table.

She caught me completely off guard as she grabbed the hair on the back of my head and shoved my face into the pile of garbage on the table. I pulled my arms up to steady myself as she kneed my side. I cringed with pain and slipped down to the level of the large wooden table. She pulled my head back again and slamed my chin into the top of the table.

Stop, you fat bitch! was all I could think to say. Then I remembered: If I yelled it loud enough, at least one of my brothers would hear it and come into the kitchen to see what was going on.

The pain from my chin and teeth rang through my head. I put my hands firmly on the top of the table to prevent her from slamming my head again. Forcefully, I turned around and faced her. The fire had now burned its way to the surface. I clenched my hand into a fist. I could tell that my fingernails had dug into the palm of my hand from the pain as I clenched tighter and tighter, trying to hold on. The muscles in my arms tightened like I was about to launch a powerful punch to her jaw. Never before had I thought about, felt like, and physically held myself back from knocking her on her ass— all at the same time.

I was about to call out some profanity at her. And she knew it. She looked me in the eyes and said: "If you wake up anybody in this house right now, I will make sure you are left behind here without a pot to piss in."

The look on her face and the magenta-red color of her neck and cheeks told me she was over the edge. She had been drinking for hours and was blowing off two weeks' worth of frustration. I knew the best thing to do was back down. I felt the anger, the frustration, and any sense of pride I had left melt out of my body. I simply stood there for a moment and watched the floor as my chin hung lower and lower until it was stuffed into my chest. Like a coward.

"Pick up all the garbage everywhere and put it back in the bags and downstairs! Especially these!" She shoved the underwear deep into the pile of garbage on the table. Without hesitation, she walked back into the kitchen, reached into the cabinet above the counter next to the stove, and pulled out yet another gallon of vodka.

Half a gallon of vodka and you're into the next one, I said to myself as I shook my head.

I picked up all the trash on the table and around the floor. I filled three trash bags with smelly garbage. When it was all cleaned up and put back in the cans downstairs, I walked back up to the kitchen. As I stood there for a moment waiting for her next command, I noticed the clock on the wall over the table. It was three fifteen in the morning. I simply turned around and walked back to my bedroom. I could hear my younger brother Keith stirring in his sleep as I climbed into the top bunk.

"You have no idea, do you? Just no idea," I whispered to him as I leaned over the rail and looked down at him.

Perhaps that's what David once said to me, I thought.

18

LETTING GO

When we experience something that changes our lives, we are sometimes left with a sense of accomplishment or even a sense of direction. Sometimes we're left with a sense of being lost and unable to find a direction to move in. What I experienced in the basement a few moments later was frightening, and yet almost spiritual. I finally faced myself and came to terms with who I had become. What I didn't know at the time was that it was the beginning of finding out just who I am now. My search was over; I had to say goodbye to that little red-haired, freckle-faced boy and let him go forever.

I CLIMBED OUT OF BED, walked quietly past the kitchen, and headed downstairs. I didn't know what I was looking for, but the basement was almost calling me. I closed my eyes and walked back to the top of the stairs. I looked back and silently closed the basement door behind me. Slowly I returned to my bedroom. Once in bed again, I felt a sense of sorrow as I thought about the basement. Time passed as I tried desperately to sleep. The basement was calling out to me. I knew deep in my heart that I had to walk down there one more time.

I was very careful not to wake Mom as I passed her room down the hallway that led to the basement door. I passed Scott's room at the bottom of the landing as quietly as I could. Once I was sure I hadn't made a sound or disturbed my sleeping brothers, I sat on the bottom of the steps and stared into the cold cement.

I knew each hole and crevice of those cement walls. Over the years, I had in some way placed a little piece of myself into each nook and hole. I was able to recall certain events and emotions from years past. I recalled sitting inches away from the concrete holding my hand flat against the cold cement looking for a sign of life in the silence of the walls. I was looking for something, but I didn't know what I wanted to find. As I stood there, holding my hand to the wall, I could see myself as a child. I was looking at myself, once so small and meek. I looked down at my hands. Now that I was a teenager, my hands were so much larger than those of the little boy.

I watched myself grow up right before my eyes. It was as if my life was a movie playing before me. I could see myself as a five-year-old boy, somehow believing that the concrete would help me hold my emotions inside. I watched myself as I walked around the basement. The concrete was like a canvas and different stages of my life were painted on the walls.

The wall behind the workbench held certain memories I had buried deep in my mind and hadn't thought about in months. I saw the many times that I hid a half sandwich in the workbench for my brother to eat. Sometimes I hid them to help him, but most of the time I hid them to get him in trouble. Feeding David was one of the worst crimes that anyone in her family—or I, for that matter—could commit.

I could see myself crawling under the shelves of the workbench where the paint cans were stored, hiding like an animal. I was trying to get away from her and once again become invisible. I watched myself sitting motionless as the spiders and bugs crawled on and around me, age five, while I hid from Mom and her drunken temper.

I continued to watch. I saw myself walk past the end of the workbench, looking into the dark corner where the trash cans and lawn mower were kept, and I was afraid. From the depths of my mind came that terrible flashback as I watched myself being lifted off the ground from the force of an eighteen-inch pipe wrench swung up in the air and into my jaw. I could feel the pain once again as I saw it slammed into my jawbone. I once again heard my skull hitting the cement as I fell to the ground. The emotions that came back to me were overwhelming. I tried desperately to clear my head. I even closed my eyes, hoping that the vision now before me would go away.

I reopened my eyes and I saw that same child, now a little older, walk over to the pile of debris next to the tall metal ladder along the far cement wall. I watched as I looked down and saw some old brown boots I used to wear. I'd taken them from a neighbor's trash pile. I hid the boots between the ladder and the wall so no one could find them. I would wear them whenever I had the chance to walk to school leaving the house through the open garage door. On my way out, I would stop and change into those old dirty boots. They were far too large, but they felt better than the shoes I had worn all year that were far too small.

Again, I closed my eyes and stood in silence. I prayed that I would see no more. I wondered if perhaps I, too, was losing my mind. For a moment I thought of Mom as she slept in her bedroom just feet above the ceiling of the basement where I now stood. I wondered if I was losing my sense of re-ality like Mom had. I sat down with my eyes closed and won-dered if I was, at fifteen, just as insane as Mom.

Anxiously I opened my eyes and watched myself, now about seven or eight, walking past the old woodshed and plac-ing half sandwiches for David in the pile of wood kept in a large cart near the far wall. The insects and dirt that covered the wood always frightened me but never stopped me. I won-dered just how many of those sandwiches my brother ate, and how many the bugs ate. I wondered how many they both ate.

I closed my eyes and wished it all away. Before I could stop them, tears rolled down my face. It was long after mid-night—probably close to dawn—and I knew I had to be very quiet. I shook my head and wiped my eyes when I saw myself at nine sitting in the corner of the garage just before sunrise watching the water from the morning dew run down the concrete walls into a pool on the floor. I felt my insides twist and bend as I saw that child reach out to the cold wall and feel the dampness from the fog, thinking that the walls cried with me from all the pain and suffering they had witnessed.

All of those memories of acts of violence were buried in my soul and the concrete walls. I felt better about holding it all in when I saw the walls cry for me, time after time.

I had carefully placed my secret emotions and fears in the holes of the concrete walls. I believed the concrete was the only thing that could hold them. When the morning dew ran down, I thought that the walls cried quietly and unnoticed like me. With tears running down my face, I saw that same child kneeling down and reaching out to the wall behind the woodshed, begging for an answer as Mom beat me.

Now I saw that child standing up to the washer and dryer, trying to reach the controls to start the machine. The pants and the same dirty shirt that I had worn for years were draped across his skinny body. The vision I watched was so real I could smell the scent of the mold from the wet clothes on the floor. I watched that dirty little boy try to wash his filthy clothes.

Just for a moment, the visions stopped. The basement was filled with an eerie silence. Everything was motionless. I could hear the blood rush through my ears. Then I saw it. I saw the place where IT used to sleep. The vision flashed before me of him in nearly no clothes, freezing and hungry, with some new bruises or marks on his skinny body. Frightened, I turned around and closed my eyes. Silently I waited and turn back. He was gone. The ghost was gone.

Before I could think about what I'd seen, I turned to the last wall, which held metal shelves and a massive collection of junk. I watched in horror as my mother shoved that little redheaded boy into the metal shelves. The sound of the shelves crashing to the cement as they fell on top of me was so real, I thought it would now wake the house. I saw myself reaching out to her, calling her name as she walked away, laughing as she left me under the crushing debris.

Then they stopped; the ghosts of my past stopped. It was silent and cold.

I realized that my entire life to this point was a mesh of tears and pain. Tears I would cry and tears I watched run down the concrete walls in the basement. I sat on the steps and cried. I must have cried for an hour before I walked up the steps toward my room. As I passed the kitchen window, I noticed that the darkness of the night was fading away. It was now just before dawn, and soon another day would start. I knew in my heart that I would never have the chance to understand what the apparitions in the basement were telling me. I didn't know what that little boy was looking for as I walked around touching the concrete walls.

Once I was back in my bunk bed, I sat and pondered what I had experienced in the basement during the night. Then I understood: What I had been looking for was myself. All those years I had been searching the concrete for an answer and didn't know it. I had walked around the basement looking into the concrete, watching that little boy see what he was and what he had now become. For the first time in years I felt comfortable and secure. I knew who I was.

I now understood who and what Mom was. I knew what I must do to end the pain, the fear, and the tears. Those tears were the only constant things in my life. Now my fear of her was gone and I felt comfortable with my decision.

I knew what I had to do.

I had thought about taking my own life many times before, but this time I knew it felt right. At fifteen, I felt no remorse or guilt; simply a calmness I had experienced a few times in my life years before. Between the calmness and the San Francisco early-morning fog, I felt complete. I leaned over and stretched across the bed with my elbows in the mattress and my palms on my cheeks as I looked out the open window. The sky changed colors from deep darkness to an orange of warmth and comfort. A comfort that I actually felt inside me.

Never before had I experienced such an understanding. It was now clear to me that the little red-haired freckle-faced boy was gone. I was now fifteen, nearly six feet tall, and about 180 pounds. I had the physical ability to stop Mom, and I hadn't understood it.

While I thought about this, I remembered the scene earlier in this same night. Mom was at the kitchen table in another drunken state of hate and inflicting the pain she was so good at, when—in a moment—I changed. It was the moment when I clenched my fist and tried to control the rage building up inside me, like a volcano ready to erupt. I could feel the anger and the sheer power of wanting to knock her across the room. For a moment I'd been ready to stand up for myself and stop the madness. But I'd backed down. Again.

That's what I couldn't understand. What had made me back down? I was older, taller, and stronger now. I could have stopped her.

Why didn't you stop her? I asked myself.

Then it hit me. As the daybreak filled my bedroom, as the sunlight came into the room and broke the darkness, it hit me.

What I was holding on to was that little boy.

I had been so desperate for Mom to love that little boy that I couldn't let him go until I found a way for Mom to love me. All the time I had spent hanging on and shrinking into that child amazed me. I recalled my thoughts about my own life and I realized that as a child, I could never have stood up to Mom and fought back.

I'm not that little boy anymore.

"He's gone now," I said aloud and with confidence.

Everything had finally fallen into its place.

I was about to leave the neighborhood I grew up in and all the people who had been part of my life up until now. I was about to start another journey, only now as a teenager. The thoughts of starting a new life in a new town with new people around me filled me with hope.

Once the sunlight reached my face and I felt the warmth of the new day, I knew what I had to do.

I looked out the window and took a deep breath. Then I sat back on my bed and quietly said good-bye to the little boy inside.

AFTERWORD

Of all the questions I'm asked, the one that surfaces over and over again is "How could this have been allowed to happen?" There is no simple answer. Rather than spending all that energy and time on wondering and trying to put the pieces together about what did happen, I'm focused on what is happening.

In today's environment, this kind of abuse could rarely go on for as long as it did. Given the amount of awareness now present in our schools, we as a community would not allow it to happen. We have come a long way since the early 1970s, and we all have seen too many events in parking lots, shopping malls, and even in our neighbors' homes that are child abuse.

Resources for children, adults, parents, and nonparents have been improved over the years, and it's made a difference. A difference that could and has changed many parents and saved many children. That's what this is all about.

This book has a particular purpose: to increase our aware-ness, and to heighten the determination of all of us as par-ents, guardians, family, and responsible adults to seek an understanding of just who we really are and to appreciate what we have as parents. Even the smallest of good and bad actions affects the smallest of us.

The value of just one soul is greater than any single thing upon this earth. For there can be nothing greater than raising a child in preparation for that journey back to where he came from, a place where his immortal father lives, a place known as heaven, a place called home.